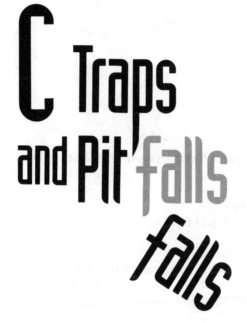

C Traps and Pitfalls

ANDREW KOENIG

AT&T Bell Laboratories

ADDISON-WESLEY PUBLISHING COMPANY
Reading, Massachusetts • Menlo Park, California • Sydney
Don Mills, Ontario • Madrid • San Juan • New York • Singapore
Amsterdam • Wokingham, England • Tokyo • Bonn

Library of Congress Cataloging-in-Publication Data

Koenig, Andrew.
   C traps and pitfalls.

   Includes index.
   1. C (Computer program language)   I. Title.
QA76.73.C15K67   1989   005.26   88-16616
ISBN 0-201-17928-8

Reprinted with corrections November , 1988

This book was typeset in Palatino and Courier by the author, using an Autologic APS-5 phototypesetter and a DEC MicroVAX II computer running the 9th Edition of the UNIX operating system.

UNIX is a registered trademark of AT&T.
DEC, PDP, and VAX are trademarks of Digital Equipment Corporation.

6 7 8 9 10 AL 9594939291

To Barbara,
who for too long
has had to endure
a house full of drafts.

Tools that are comfortable after experience are often more difficult to learn at first than those that feel right immediately. Student pilots start out overcontrolling, turning first flights into roller-coaster rides, until they learn how light a touch flying really requires. Training wheels on a bicycle make it easier for a novice to ride, but get in the way after that.

So it is also with programming languages. Every programming language has aspects that are most likely to cause trouble for people not yet thoroughly familiar with them. These aspects vary from one language to another, but are surprisingly constant from one programmer to another. Thus the idea of collecting them.

My first effort to collect such problems was in 1977, when I gave a talk called *PL/I Traps and Pitfalls* at the SHARE (IBM mainframe users' group) meeting in Washington DC. That was shortly after I moved from Columbia University, where people used PL/I heavily, to AT&T Bell Laboratories, where people use C heavily. The decade that followed gave me ample experience in how C programmers (including me) can get themselves into trouble if they're not certain of what they're doing.

I started collecting C problems in 1985 and published the collection as an internal paper at the end of that year. The response astonished me: more than 2,000 people requested copies of the paper from the Bell Labs library. That convinced me to expand the paper into this book.

What this book is

C Traps and Pitfalls aims to encourage defensive programming by showing how other people, even experienced professionals, have gotten themselves into trouble. These mistakes are generally easy to avoid once seen and understood, so the emphasis is on specific examples rather than generalities.

This book belongs on your shelf if you are using C at all seriously, even if you are an expert: many of the professional C programmers who saw early drafts said things like "that bug bit me just last week!" If you are teaching a course that uses C, it belongs at the top of your supplementary reading list.

What this book is not

This book is not a criticism of C. Programmers can get themselves into trouble in any language. I have tried here to distill a decade of C experience into a compact form in the hope that you, the reader, will be able to avoid some of the stupid mistakes I've made and seen others make.

This book is not a cookbook. Errors cannot be avoided by recipe. If they could, we could eliminate automobile accidents by plastering the countryside with *Drive Carefully* signs! People learn most effectively through experience — their own or someone else's. Merely understanding how a particular kind of mistake is possible is a big step on the way to avoiding it in the future.

This book is not intended to teach you how to program in C (see Kernighan and Ritchie: *The C Programming Language*, second edition, Prentice-Hall 1988), nor is it a reference manual (see Harbison and Steele: *C: A Reference Manual*, second edition, Prentice-Hall 1987). It does not mention algorithms or data structures (see Van Wyk: *Data Structures and C Programs*, Addison-Wesley 1988), and only briefly discusses portability (see Horton: *How to Write Portable Programs in C*, Prentice-Hall 1989) and operating system interfaces (see Kernighan and Pike: *The UNIX Programming Environment*, Prentice-Hall 1984). The problems mentioned are real, although often shortened (for a collection of composed C problems see Feuer: *The C Puzzle Book*, Prentice-Hall 1982). It is neither a dictionary nor an encyclopedia; I have kept it short to encourage you to read it all.

Your name in lights

I'm sure I've missed some pitfalls. If you find one I've missed, please contact me via Addison-Wesley. I may well include your discovery, with an acknowledgment, in a future edition.

A word about ANSI C

As I write this, the ANSI C standard is not yet final. It is technically incorrect to refer to "ANSI C" until the ANSI committee finishes its work. In practice, though, the ANSI standard is far enough along that nothing I say about ANSI C is likely to change. C compilers are already available that implement many of the significant improvements contemplated by the ANSI committee.

Don't worry if your C implementation does not support the ANSI function syntax mentioned here: it is easy enough to understand the parts of the examples where it matters, and you can fall into the traps described there regardless of what version of C you use.

Acknowledgments

A collection like this could not possibly have been made in isolation. People who have pointed out particular pitfalls include Steve Bellovin (§6.3, p.82), Mark Brader (§1.1, p.6), Luca Cardelli (§4.4, p.62), Larry Cipriani (§2.3, p.21), Guy Harris and Steve Johnson (§2.2, p.20), Phil Karn (§2.2, p.17), Dave Kristol (§7.5, p.90), George W. Leach (§1.1, p.7), Doug McIlroy (§2.3, p.21), Barbara Moo (§7.2, p.88), Rob Pike (§1.1, p.6), Jim Reeds (§3.6, p.36), Dennis Ritchie (§2.2, p.19), Janet Sirkis (§5.2, p.70), Richard Stevens (§2.5, p.24), Bjarne Stroustrup (§2.3, p.20), Ephraim Vishniac (§1.4, p.9), and one contributor who wishes to remain anonymous (§2.3, p.22). For brevity, I've mentioned only the first person to report any particular problem to me. Of course, I doubt any of the people I've mentioned actually *invented* the programming errors they pointed out to me, and if they did I doubt they'd admit it! I know I've made many of them myself too, some several times.

Useful editorial suggestions came from Steve Bellovin, Jim Coplien, Marc Donner, Jon Forrest, Brian Kernighan, Doug McIlroy, Barbara Moo, Rob Murray, Bob Richton, Dennis Ritchie, Jonathan Shapiro, and several anonymous reviewers. Lee McMahon and Ed Sitar pointed out what would otherwise have been embarrassing typographical errors in early drafts of the manuscript. Dave Prosser clarified many fine points of ANSI C for me. Brian Kernighan supplied invaluable typesetting tools and assistance.

It has been a delight to work with the people at Addison-Wesley, including Jim DeWolf, Mary Dyer, Lorraine Ferrier, Katherine Harutunian, Marshall Henrichs, Debbie Lafferty, Keith Wollman, and Helen Wythe. I'm sure they've gained from the aid of others whom I haven't met.

I am particularly grateful to the enlightened managers at AT&T Bell Laboratories who made it possible for me to write this book at all, including Steve Chappell, Bob Factor, Wayne Hunt, Rob Murray, Will Smith, Dan Stanzione, and Eric Sumner.

The title of this book was suggested by Robert Sheckley's science-fiction anthology *The People Trap and Other Pitfalls, Snares, Devices, and Delusions (as well as two Sniggles and a Contrivance)*, published by Dell Books in 1968.

CONTENTS

0 Introduction 1

1 Lexical pitfalls 5
  1.1   = is not == 6
  1.2   & and ¦ are not && or ¦¦ 7
  1.3   Greedy lexical analysis 7
  1.4   Integer constants 9
  1.5   Strings and characters 10

2 Syntactic pitfalls 13
  2.1   Understanding function declarations 13
  2.2   Operators don't always have the precedence you want 17
  2.3   Watch those semicolons! 20
  2.4   The switch statement 22
  2.5   Calling functions 24
  2.6   The dangling else problem 24

3 Semantic pitfalls 27
  3.1   Pointers and arrays 27
  3.2   Pointers are not arrays 32
  3.3   Array declarations as parameters 33
  3.4   Eschew synecdoche 34
  3.5   Null pointers are not null strings 35
  3.6   Counting and asymmetric bounds 36
  3.7   Order of evaluation 46
  3.8   The &&, ¦¦, and ! operators 48
  3.9   Integer overflow 49
  3.10 Returning a value from main 50

4 Linkage..**53**

    4.1   What is a linker?...53

    4.2   Declarations vs. definitions.......................................54

    4.3   Name conflicts and the `static` modifier 56

    4.4   Arguments, parameters, and return values 57

    4.5   Checking external types 63

    4.6   Header files 66

5 Library functions **69**

    5.1   `getchar` returns an integer 70

    5.2   Updating a sequential file..70

    5.3   Buffered output and memory allocation.................72

    5.4   Using `errno` for error detection..............................73

    5.5   The `signal` function...74

6 The preprocessor **77**

    6.1   Spaces matter in macro definitions...........................77

    6.2   Macros are not functions...78

    6.3   Macros are not statements..82

    6.4   Macros are not type definitions 83

7 Portability pitfalls **85**

    7.1   Coping with change...85

    7.2   What's in a name?..87

    7.3   How big is an integer? 88

    7.4   Are characters signed or unsigned?.........................89

    7.5   Shift operators...90

    7.6   Memory location zero 91

    7.7   How does division truncate? 92

    7.8   How big is a random number?...................................93

    7.9   Case conversion 93

   7.10   Free first, then reallocate?..95

   7.11   An example of portability problems.........................96

8 Advice and answers...**101**

    8.1   Advice..102

    8.2   Answers...105

Appendix: `printf, varargs,` **and** `stdarg` 121
    A.1   The `printf` family...121
          Simple format types 123
          Modifiers...127
          Flags...130
          Variable field width and precision.....................................132
          Neologisms 133
          Anachronisms..133
    A.2   Variable argument lists with `varargs.h`............................134
          Implementing `varargs.h`..138
    A.3   `stdarg.h:` the ANSI `varargs.h`...139

I wrote my first computer program in 1966, in Fortran. I had intended it to compute and print the Fibonacci numbers up to 10,000: the elements of the sequence 1, 1, 2, 3, 5, 8, 13, 21, ..., with each number after the second being the sum of the two preceding ones. Of course it didn't work:

```
      I = 0
      J = 0
      K = 1
  1 PRINT 10, K
      I = J
      J = K
      K = I + J
      IF (K - 10000) 1, 1, 2
  2 CALL EXIT
 10 FORMAT (I10)
```

Fortran programmers will find it obvious that this program is missing an END statement. Once I added the END statement, though, the program still didn't compile, producing the mysterious message ERROR   6.

   Careful reading of the manual eventually revealed the problem: the Fortran compiler I was using would not handle integer constants with more than four digits. Changing 10000 to 9999 solved the problem.

   I wrote my first C program in 1977. Of course it didn't work:

```
#include <stdio.h>

main()
{
        printf("Hello world");
}
```

This program compiled on the first try. Its result was a little peculiar, though: the terminal output looked somewhat like this:

```
% cc prog.c
% a.out
Hello world%
```

Here the % character is the system's *prompt*, which is the string the system uses to tell me it is my turn to type. The % appears immediately after the Hello world message because I forgot to tell the system to begin a new line afterwards. Section 3.10 (page 51) discusses an even subtler error in this program.

There is a real difference between these two kinds of problem. The Fortran example contained two errors, but the implementation was good enough to point them out. The C program was technically correct — from the machine's viewpoint it contained no errors. Hence there were no diagnostic messages. The machine did exactly what I told it; it just didn't do quite what I had in mind.

This book concentrates on the second kind of problem: programs that don't do what the programmer might have expected. More than that, it will concentrate on ways to slip up that are peculiar to C. For example, consider this program fragment to initialize an integer array with N elements:

```
int i;
int a[N];
for (i = 0; i <= N; i++)
        a[i] = 0;
```

On many C implementations, this program will go into an infinite loop! Section 3.6 (page 36) shows why.

Programming errors represent places where a program departs from the programmer's mental model of that program. By their very nature they are thus hard to classify. I have tried to group them according to their relevance to various ways of looking at a program.

At a low level, a program is as a sequence of *symbols*, or *tokens*, just as a book is a sequence of words. The process of separating a program into symbols is called *lexical analysis*. Chapter 1 looks at problems that stem from the way C lexical analysis is done.

One can view the tokens that make up a program as a sequence of statements and declarations, just as one can view a book as a collection of sentences. In both cases, the meaning comes from the details of how tokens or words are combined into larger units. Chapter 2 treats errors that can arise from misunderstanding these *syntactic* details.

Chapter 3 deals with misconceptions of meaning: ways a programmer who intended to say one thing can actually be saying something else. We assume here that the lexical and syntactic details of the language are well understood and concentrate on *semantic* details.

Chapter 4 recognizes that a C program is often made out of several parts that are compiled separately and later bound together. This process is called *linkage* and is part of the relationship between the program and its environment.

That environment includes some set of *library routines*. Although not strictly part of the language, library routines are essential to any C program that does anything useful. In particular, a few library routines are used by almost every C program, and there are enough ways to go wrong using them to merit the discussion in Chapter 5.

Chapter 6 notes that the program we write is not really the program we run; the preprocessor has gotten at it first. Although various preprocessor implementations differ somewhat, we can say useful things about aspects that many implementations have in common.

Chapter 7 discusses portability problems — reasons a program might run on one implementation and not another. It is surprisingly hard to do even simple things like integer arithmetic correctly.

Chapter 8 offers advice in defensive programming and answers the exercises from the other chapters.

Finally, an Appendix covers three common but widely misunderstood library facilities.

Exercise 0-1. Would you buy an automobile made by a company with a high proportion of recalls? Would that change if they told you they had cleaned up their act? What does it *really* cost for your users to find your bugs for you? □

Exercise 0-2. How many fence posts 10 feet apart do you need to support 100 feet of fence? □

Exercise 0-3. Have you ever cut yourself with a knife while cooking? How could cooking knives be made safer? Would you want to use a knife that had been modified that way? □

When we read a sentence, we do not usually think about the meaning of the individual letters of the words that make it up. Indeed, letters mean little by themselves: we group them into words and assign meanings to those words.

So it is also with programs in C and other languages. The individual characters of the program do not mean anything in isolation but only in context. Thus in

```
p->s = "->";
```

the two instances of the – character mean two different things. More precisely, each instance of – is part of a different *token:* the first is part of -> and the second is part of a character string. Moreover, the -> token has a meaning quite distinct from that of either of the characters that make it up.

The word *token* refers to a part of a program that plays much the same role as a word in a sentence: in some sense it means the same thing every time it appears. The same sequence of characters can belong to one token in one context and an entirely different token in another context. The part of a compiler that breaks a program up into tokens is often called a *lexical analyzer*.

For another example, consider the statement:

```
if (x > big) big = x;
```

The first token in this statement is if, a keyword. The next token is the left parenthesis, followed by the identifier x, the "greater than" symbol, the identifier big, and so on. In C, we can always insert extra space (blanks, tabs, or newlines) between tokens, so we could have written:

```
if
(
x
>
big
)
big
=
x
;
```

This chapter will explore some common misunderstandings about the meanings of tokens and the relationship between tokens and the characters that make them up.

1.1   = is not ==

Most programming languages derived from Algol, such as Pascal and Ada, use := for assignment and = for comparison. C, on the other hand, uses = for assignment and == for comparison. This is convenient: assignment is more frequent than comparison, so the shorter symbol is written more often. Moreover, C treats assignment as an operator, so that multiple assignments (such as a=b=c) can be written easily and assignments can be embedded in larger expressions.

This convenience causes a potential problem: one can inadvertently write an assignment where one intended a comparison. Thus, the following statement, which apparently executes a break if x is equal to y:

```
if (x = y)
        break;
```

actually sets x to the value of y and then checks whether that value is nonzero. Or consider the following loop, which is intended to skip blanks, tabs, and newlines in a file:

```
while (c = ' ' || c == '\t' || c == '\n')
        c = getc(f);
```

This loop mistakenly uses = instead of == in the comparison with ' '. Because the = operator has lower precedence than the || operator, the "comparison" actually assigns to c the value of the entire expression

```
' ' || c == '\t' || c == '\n'
```

The value of ' ' is nonzero, so this expression evaluates to 1 regardless of the (previous) value of c. Thus the loop will eat the entire file. What it does after that depends on whether the particular implementation allows a program to keep reading after it has reached end of file. If it does, the loop will run forever.

Some C compilers try to help their users by giving a warning message for conditions of the form *e1* = *e2*. When assigning a value to a variable and then checking whether the variable is zero, consider making the comparison explicit to avoid warning messages from such compilers. In other words, instead of

```
if (x = y)
        foo();
```

write:

```
if ((x = y) != 0)
        foo();
```

This will also help make your intentions plain. We'll talk in Section 2.2 (page 17) about why the parentheses are needed around x = y.

It is possible to confuse matters in the other direction too:

```
if ((filedesc == open(argv[i], 0)) < 0)
        error();
```

The open function in this example returns −1 if it detects an error and zero or a positive number if it succeeds. This fragment is intended to store the result of open in filedesc and check for success at the same time. However, the first == should be =. As written, it compares filedesc with the result of open and checks whether the result of that comparison is negative. Of course it never is: the result of == is always 0 or 1 and never negative. Thus error is not called. Everything appears normal but the value of filedesc is whatever it was before, which has nothing to do with the result of open. Some compilers might warn that the comparison with 0 has no effect, but you shouldn't count on it.

1.2   & and ¦ are not && or ¦¦

It is easy to miss an inadvertent substitution of = for == because so many other languages use = for comparison. It is also easy to interchange & and &&, or ¦ and ¦¦, especially because the & and ¦ operators in C are different from their counterparts in some other languages. Section 3.8 (page 48) will discuss the precise meanings of these operators.

1.3   Greedy lexical analysis

Some C tokens, such as /, *, and =, are only one character long. Other C tokens, such as /*, ==, and identifiers, are several characters long. When a C compiler encounters a / followed by an *, it must be able to decide whether to treat these two characters as two separate tokens or as one single token. C resolves this question with a simple rule: *repeatedly bite off the biggest possible piece.* That is, the way to convert a C program to tokens is to move from left to right, taking the longest possible token each time. This strategy is also sometimes referred to as *greedy*, or, more colloquially, as the *maximal munch* strategy. Kernighan and Ritchie put it this way: "If the input stream has been parsed into tokens up to a given character, the next token is taken to include the longest string of characters which could possibly constitute a token." Tokens (except string or character constants) never contain embedded white space (blanks, tabs, or newlines).

Thus, for instance, == is a single token, = = is two, and the expression

```
a---b
```

means the same as

```
a -- - b
```

rather than

```
a - -- b
```

Similarly, if a / is the first character of a token, and the / is immediately followed by *, the two characters begin a comment, *regardless* of any other context.

The following statement looks like it sets y to the value of x divided by the value pointed to by p:

```
y = x/*p    /* p points at the divisor */;
```

In fact, /* begins a comment, so the compiler will simply gobble program text until the */ appears. In other words, the statement just sets y to the value of x and doesn't even look at p. Rewriting this statement as

```
y = x / *p    /* p points at the divisor */;
```

or even

```
y = x/(*p)    /* p points at the divisor */;
```

would cause it to do the division the comment suggests.

This sort of near-ambiguity can cause trouble in other contexts. For example, at one time C used =+ to mean what is presently denoted by +=. Some C compilers still accept the archaic usage; such a compiler will treat

```
a=-1;
```

as meaning

```
a =- 1;
```

which means the same thing as

```
a = a - 1;
```

This will surprise a programmer who intended

```
a = -1;
```

This kind of archaic compiler would also treat

```
a=/*b;
```

as

```
a =/ * b ;
```

even though the /* looks like a comment.

Such older compilers also treat compound assignments as two tokens. Such a compiler will handle

```
a >> = 1;
```

with no problem but a strict ANSI C compiler will reject it.

1.4   Integer constants

If the first character of an integer constant is the digit 0, that constant is taken to be in octal. Thus 10 and 010 mean very different things. Moreover, many C compilers accept 8 and 9 as "octal" digits without complaint. The meaning of this strange construct follows from the definition of octal numbers. For instance, 0195 means $1 \times 8^2 + 9 \times 8^1 + 5 \times 8^0$, which is equivalent to 141 (decimal) or 0215 (octal). Obviously we recommend against such usage. ANSI C prohibits it.

Watch out for inadvertent octal values in contexts like this:

```
struct {
        int part_number;
        char *description;
} parttab[] = {
        046,    "left-handed widget"    ,
        047,    "right-handed widget"   ,
        125,    "frammis"
};
```

1.5   Strings and characters

Single and double quotes mean very different things in C, and confusing them in some contexts will result in surprises rather than error messages.

A character enclosed in single quotes is just another way of writing the   integer   that   corresponds   to   the   given   character   in   the implementation's collating sequence. Thus, in an ASCII implementation, 'a' means exactly the same thing as 0141 or 97.

A string enclosed in double quotes, on the other hand, is a short-hand way of writing a pointer to the initial character of a nameless array that has been initialized with the characters between the quotes and an extra character whose binary value is zero.

Thus the statement

```
printf("Hello world\n");
```

is equivalent to

```
char hello[] = {'H', 'e', 'l', 'l', 'o', ' ',
        'w', 'o', 'r', 'l', 'd', '\n', 0};
printf(hello);
```

Because a character in single quotes represents an integer and a character in double quotes represents a pointer, compiler type checking will usually catch places where one is used for the other. Thus, for example, saying

```
char *slash = '/';
```

will yield an error message because '/' is not a character pointer. However, some implementations don't check argument types, particularly arguments to printf. Thus, saying

```
printf('\n');
```

instead of

```
printf("\n");
```

may result in a surprise at run time instead of a compiler diagnostic. Section 4.4 (page 57) discusses other cases in detail.

Because an integer is usually large enough to hold several characters, some C compilers permit multiple characters in a character constant as well as a string constant. This means that writing 'yes' instead of "yes" may well go undetected. The latter means "the address of the first of four consecutive memory locations containing y, e, s, and a null character, respectively." The meaning of 'yes' is not precisely defined, but many C implementations take it to mean "an integer that is composed somehow of the values of the characters y, e, and s." Any similarity between these two quantities is purely coincidental.

Exercise 1-1. Some C compilers allow nested comments. Write a C program that finds out if it is being run on such a compiler *without* any error messages. In other words, the program should be valid under both comment rules, but should do different things in each. *Hint.* A comment symbol /* inside a quoted string is just part of the string; a double quote "" inside a comment is part of the comment. □

Exercise 1-2. If you were writing a C compiler, would you make it possible for users to nest comments? If you were using a C compiler that permitted nested comments, would you use that facility? Does your answer to the second question affect your answer to the first? □

Exercise 1-3. Why does n-->0 mean n-- > 0 and not n- -> 0? □

Exercise 1-4. What does a+++++b mean? □

CHAPTER 2: **SYNTACTIC PITFALLS**

To understand a C program, it is not enough to understand the tokens that make it up. One must also understand how the tokens combine to form declarations, expressions, statements, and programs. While these combinations are usually well-defined, the definitions are sometimes counter-intuitive or confusing. This chapter looks at some syntactic constructions that are less than obvious.

2.1 Understanding function declarations

I once talked to someone who was writing a C program to run stand-alone in a microprocessor. When this machine was switched on, the hardware would call the subroutine whose address was stored in location zero.

In order to simulate turning power on, we had to devise a C statement that would call this subroutine explicitly. After some thought, we came up with the following:

```
(*(void(*)())0)();
```

Expressions like these strike terror into the hearts of C programmers. They needn't, though, because they can usually be constructed quite easily with the help of a single, simple rule: *declare it the way you use it.*

Every C variable declaration has two parts: a type and a list of expression-like things called *declarators*. A declarator looks something like an expression that is expected to evaluate to the given type. The simplest declarator is a variable:

```
float f, g;
```

indicates that the expressions f and g, when evaluated, will be of type float. Because a declarator looks like an expression, parentheses may be used freely:

```
float ((f));
```

means that ((f)) evaluates to a float and therefore, by inference, that f is also a float.

Similar logic applies to function and pointer types. For example,

```
float ff();
```

means that the expression ff() is a float, and therefore that ff is a function that returns a float. Analogously,

```
float *pf;
```

means that *pf is a float and therefore that pf is a pointer to a float.

These forms combine in declarations the same way they do in expressions. Thus

```
float *g(), (*h)();
```

says that *g() and (*h)() are float expressions. Since () binds more tightly than *, *g() means the same thing as *(g()): g is a function that returns a pointer to a float, and h is a pointer to a function that returns a float.

Once we know how to declare a variable of a given type, it is easy to write a cast for that type: just remove the variable name and the semicolon from the declaration and enclose the whole thing in parentheses. Thus, since

```
float (*h)();
```

declares h to be a pointer to a function returning a float,

```
(float (*)())
```

is a cast to a pointer to a function returning a float.

We can now analyze the expression (*(void(*)())0)() in two stages.

First, suppose that we have a variable fp that contains a function pointer and we want to call the function to which fp points. That is done this way:

```
(*fp)();
```

If fp is a pointer to a function, *fp is the function itself, so (*fp)() is the way to invoke it. ANSI C permits this to be abbreviated as fp(), but keep in mind that it is only an abbreviation.

The parentheses around *fp in the expression (*fp)() are essential because function application binds more tightly than unary operators. Without parentheses *fp() means precisely the same as *(fp()). ANSI C treats this as an abbreviation for *((*fp)()).

We have now reduced the problem to that of finding an appropriate expression to replace fp. This problem is the second part of our analysis. If C could read our mind about types, we could write:

```
(*0)();
```

This doesn't work because the * operator insists on having a pointer as its operand. Furthermore, the operand must be a pointer to a function so that the result of * can be called. Thus, we need to cast 0 into a type loosely described as "pointer to function returning void."

If fp is a pointer to a function returning void, then (*fp)() is a void value, and its declaration would look like this:

```
void (*fp)();
```

Thus, we could write:

```
void (*fp)();
(*fp)();
```

at the cost of declaring a dummy variable. But once we know how to declare the variable, we know how to cast a constant to that type: just drop the name from the variable declaration. Thus, we cast 0 to a "pointer to function returning void" by saying:

```
(void(*)())0
```

and we can now replace fp by (void(*)())0:

```
(*(void(*)())0)();
```

The semicolon on the end turns the expression into a statement.

At the time I tackled this problem, there was no such thing as a typedef declaration. Although going through this example without typedef is a good way to expose the details, typedef makes it clearer:

```
typedef void (*funcptr)();
(*(funcptr)0)();
```

This messy example has relatives that C programmers may meet more often. Consider, for example, the signal library function. In C implementations that include this function, it takes two arguments: an integer code representing the particular signal to be trapped, and a pointer to a user-supplied function, returning void, to handle that signal. Section 5.5 (page 74) discusses this function in more detail.

Programmers do not generally declare the signal function themselves. Instead, they rely on a declaration from the system header file signal.h. How does that header file declare the signal function?

It is easiest to start by thinking about the user-defined signal handler function, which might be defined this way:

```
void
sigfunc(int n)
{
        /* signals handled here */
}
```

The argument to `sigfunc` is an integer representing a signal number; we will ignore it for now.

The (hypothetical) function body above defines `sigfunc`. To declare it, we would write:

```
void sigfunc(int);
```

Now assume we want to declare `sfp` as a variable that might point to `sigfunc`. If `sfp` points to `sigfunc`, then `*sfp` must represent `sigfunc` itself, and hence `*sfp` is callable. Then if `sig` is an int, `(*sfp)(sig)` is a `void`, so we declare `sfp` this way:

```
void (*sfp)(int);
```

This shows how to declare `signal`. Since `signal` returns a value of the same type as `sfp`, we must be able to declare it this way:

```
void (*signal(something))(int);
```

The *something* here represents the types of `signal`'s arguments, which we must still understand how to write. One way to read this declaration is to treat it as saying that calling `signal` with appropriate arguments, dereferencing the result, and then calling that with an int argument gives a void. Thus `signal` must be a function that returns a pointer to a function returning `void`.

What about the arguments to `signal` itself? We want to say that `signal` accepts two arguments: an int signal number and a pointer to a user-defined signal handler function. Originally we declared a pointer to a signal handler function by saying

```
void (*sfp)(int);
```

The type of `sfp` is obtained by dropping `sfp` from its declaration to obtain `void(*)(int)`. Moreover, the `signal` function returns a pointer to the previous handler for that signal type; this pointer is also an `sfp`. Thus we can declare the `signal` function by saying:

```
void (*signal(int,void(*)(int)))(int);
```

Again, `typedef` declarations can simplify this:

```
typedef void (*HANDLER)(int);
HANDLER signal(int,HANDLER);
```

2.2 Operators don't always have the precedence you want

Suppose that the defined constant FLAG is an integer with exactly one bit turned on in its binary representation (in other words, a power of two), and you want to test whether the integer variable flags has that bit turned on. The usual way to write this is:

```
if (flags & FLAG) ...
```

The meaning of this is plain to most C programmers: an if statement tests whether the expression in the parentheses evaluates to 0 or not. It might be nice to make this test more explicit for documentation purposes:

```
if (flags & FLAG != 0) ...
```

The statement is now easier to understand. It is also wrong, because != binds more tightly than &, so the interpretation is now:

```
if (flags & (FLAG != 0)) ...
```

This will work (by coincidence) if FLAG is 1 but not otherwise.

Suppose you have two integer variables, hi and low, whose values are between 0 and 15 inclusive, and you want to set an integer r to an 8-bit value whose low-order bits are those of low and whose high-order bits are those of hi. The natural way to do this is to write:

```
r = hi<<4 + low;
```

Unfortunately, this is wrong. Addition binds more tightly than shifting, so this example is equivalent to:

```
r = hi << (4 + low);
```

Here are two ways to get it right. The second suggests that the real problem comes from mixing arithmetic and logical operations; the relative precedence of shift and logical operators is more intuitive:

```
r = (hi << 4) + low;
r = hi << 4 | low;
```

One way to avoid these problems is to parenthesize everything, but expressions with too many parentheses are hard to understand. Thus it may be useful to try to remember the precedence levels in C.

Unfortunately, there are fifteen of them, so this not always easy. The complete table appears below.

We can make this table easier to remember by classifying the operators

operator	associativity
( )　[ ]　->　.	left
!　~　++　--　-　(type)　*　&　sizeof	right
*　/　%	left
+　-	left
<<　>>	left
<　<=　>　>=	left
==　!=	left
&	left
^	left
¦	left
&&	left
¦¦	left
?:	right
assignments	right
,	left

Operator precedence table.

(operators near the top bind most tightly)

into groups and understanding the motivation for the relative precedence of the groups.

The things that bind the most tightly are the ones that aren't really operators: subscripting, function calls, and structure selection. These all associate to the left: a.b.c means the same as (a.b).c and not a.(b.c).

Next come the unary operators. These have the highest precedence of any of the true operators. Because function calls bind more tightly than unary operators, you must write (*p)() to call a function pointed to by p; *p() means the same thing as *(p()). Casts are unary operators and have the same precedence as any other unary operator. Unary operators are right-associative, so *p++ is interpreted as *(p++) (fetch the object pointed to by p and later increment p) and not as (*p)++ (increment the object pointed to by p). Section 3.7 (page 46) points out that the precise meaning of p++ can sometimes be surprising.

Next come the true binary operators. The arithmetic operators have the highest precedence, then the shift operators, the relational operators, the logical operators, the assignment operators, and finally the conditional operator. The two most important things to keep in mind are:

1. Every logical operator has lower precedence than every relational operator.

2. The shift operators bind more tightly than the relational operators but less tightly than the arithmetic operators.

Within the various operator classes, there are few surprises. Multiplication, division, and remainder have the same precedence, addition and subtraction have the same precedence, and the two shift operators have the same precedence. Some people may be surprised to find that 1/2*a means $\frac{1}{2} \times a$ and not $\frac{1}{2 \times a}$, but C behaves the same way in this respect as Fortran, Pascal, and most other programming languages.

One small surprise is that the six relational operators do not all have the same precedence: == and != bind less tightly than the other relational operators. This allows us, for instance, to see if a and b are in the same relative order as c and d by the expression

```
a < b == c < d
```

Within the logical operators, no two have the same precedence. The bitwise operators all bind more tightly than the sequential operators, each *and* operator binds more tightly than the corresponding *or* operator, and the bitwise *exclusive or* operator ^ falls between bitwise *and* and bitwise *or*.

The precedence of these operators comes about for historical reasons. B, the predecessor of C, had logical operators that corresponded roughly to C's & and ¦ operators. Although they were defined to act on bits, the compiler would treat them as the present && and ¦¦ operators if they were used in a conditional context. When the two usages were split apart in C, it was deemed too dangerous to change the precedence much.

The ternary conditional operator has lower precedence than any we have mentioned so far. This permits the selection expression to contain logical combinations of relational operators, as in

```
tax_rate = income > 40000 && residency < 5? 3.5: 2.0;
```

This example also shows that it makes sense for assignment to have a lower precedence than the conditional operator. Moreover, all the assignment operators have the same precedence and they all group right to left, so that:

```
home_score = visitor_score = 0;
```

means the same as

```
visitor_score = 0;
home_score = visitor_score;
```

Lowest of all is the comma operator. This is easy to remember because the comma is often used as a substitute for the semicolon when an expression is required instead of a statement. The comma operator is particularly useful in macro definitions (see Section 6.3 (page 82) for further discussion of this).

The assignment operator is often involved in precedence mixups. Consider, for example, the following loop intended to copy one file to another:

```
while (c=getc(in) != EOF)
        putc(c,out);
```

The expression in the while statement looks like c should be assigned the value of getc(in) and then compared with EOF to terminate the loop. Unhappily, assignment has lower precedence than any comparison operator, so the value of c will be the result of comparing getc(in), the value of which is then discarded, and EOF. Thus, the "copy" of the file will consist of a stream of bytes each of which has the (binary) value 1.

The example above should be written:

```
while ((c=getc(in)) != EOF)
        putc(c,out);
```

Errors of this sort can be hard to spot in more complicated expressions. For example, one version of the lint program mentioned in Section 4.0 (page 53) was distributed with the following erroneous line:

```
if( (t=BTYPE(pt1->aty)==STRTY) || t==UNIONTY ){
```

This was intended to assign a value to t and then see if t is equal to STRTY or UNIONTY. The actual effect is quite different: t gets the value 1 or 0 depending on whether BTYPE(pt1->aty) is equal to STRTY; if t is zero, t is then compared with UNIONTY.

2.3   Watch those semicolons!

An extra semicolon in a C program may be harmless: it might be a null statement, which has no effect, or it might elicit a diagnostic message from the compiler, which makes it easy to remove. One important exception is after an if or while clause, which must be followed by exactly one statement. Consider this example:

```
if (x[i] > big);
        big = x[i];
```

The compiler will happily digest the semicolon on the first line and because of it will treat this program fragment as something quite different from:

```
if (x[i] > big)
        big = x[i];
```

The first example is equivalent to:

```
if (x[i] > big)  { }
big = x[i];
```

which is, of course, equivalent to:†

```
big = x[i];
```

Leaving out a semicolon can cause quiet trouble too:

```
if (n < 3)
        return
logrec.date = x[0];
logrec.time = x[1];
logrec.code = x[2];
```

Here the `return` statement is missing a semicolon; yet this fragment may well compile without error, treating the entire statement

```
logrec.date = x[0];
```

as if it were the operand of the `return` statement. It is the same as:

```
if (n < 3)
        return logrec.date = x[0];
logrec.time = x[1];
logrec.code = x[2];
```

If this fragment were part of a function declared to return void, one would expect the compiler to flag it as an error. However, functions that don't return a value are often written with no return type at all, implicitly returning an int. Thus this error may go undetected. Its effect is insidious: if $n \geqslant 3$, the first of the three assignment statements is simply skipped.

Another place that a semicolon can make a big difference is at the end of a declaration just before a function definition. Consider the following fragment:

---

† Unless x, i, or big is a macro with side effects.

```
struct logrec {
        int date;
        int time;
        int code;
}

main()
{
        . . .
}
```

There is a semicolon missing between the first } and the definition of main that immediately follows it. The effect of this is to declare that the function main returns a struct logrec, which is defined as part of this declaration. Think of it this way:

```
struct logrec {
        int date;
        int time;
        int code;
} main()
{
        . . .
}
```

If the semicolon were present, main would be defined by default as returning an int.

The effect of returning a struct logrec from main instead of an int is left as an exercise in morbid imagination.

2.4 The switch statement

C is unusual in that the cases in its switch statement can flow into each other. Consider, for example, the following program fragments in C and Pascal:

```
switch (color) {
case 1: printf("red");
        break;
case 2: printf("yellow");
        break;
case 3: printf("blue");
        break;
}
```

```
case color of
1:      write('red');
2:      write('yellow');
3:      write('blue')
end
```

Both these program fragments do the same thing: print red, yellow, or blue (without starting a new line), depending on whether the variable color is 1, 2, or 3. The program fragments are exactly analogous, with one exception: the Pascal program does not have any part that corresponds to the C break statement. The reason for that is that case labels in C behave as true labels, in that control flows unimpeded right through a case label. In Pascal, on the other hand, every case label implicitly ends the previous case.

Viewing it another way, suppose the C fragment looked more like the Pascal fragment:

```
switch (color) {
case 1: printf("red");
case 2: printf("yellow");
case 3: printf("blue");
}
```

and suppose further that color were equal to 2. Then the program would print

```
yellowblue
```

because control would pass naturally from the second printf call to the statement after it.

This is both a strength and a weakness of C switch statements. It is a weakness because leaving out a break statement is easy and often gives rise to obscure program misbehavior. It is a strength because by leaving out a break statement deliberately, one can readily express a control structure that is inconvenient to implement otherwise. Specifically, in large switch statements, one often finds that the processing for one of the cases reduces to some other case after relatively little special handling.

For example, consider a program that is an interpreter for some kind of imaginary machine. Such a program might contain a switch statement to handle each of the various operation codes. On such a machine, it is often true that a subtract operation is identical to an add operation after the sign of the second operand has been inverted. Thus, it is nice to be able to write something like this:

```
case SUBTRACT:
        opnd2 = -opnd2;
        /* no break */
case ADD:
        . . .
```

Of course, a comment such as the one in the example above is a good idea; it lets the reader know that the lack of a **break** statement is intentional.

As another example, consider the part of a compiler that skips white space while looking for a token. Here, one would want to treat spaces, tabs, and newlines identically except that a newline should cause a line counter to be incremented:

```
case '\n':
        linecount++;
        /* no break */
case '\t':
case ' ':
        . . .
```

2.5 Calling functions

Unlike some other programming languages, C requires a function call to have an argument list even if there are no arguments. Thus, if **f** is a function,

```
f();
```

is a statement that calls the function, but

```
f;
```

does nothing at all. More precisely, it evaluates the address of the function but does not call it.

2.6 The dangling **else** problem

Although this well-known problem is not unique to C, it has bitten C programmers with many years of experience.

Consider the following program fragment:

```
if (x == 0)
        if (y == 0) error();
else {
        z = x + y;
        f(&z);
}
```

The programmer's intention for this fragment is that there should be two main cases: $x=0$ and $x\neq0$. In the first case, the fragment should do nothing at all unless $y=0$, in which case it should call error. In the second case, the program should set z to x+y and then call f with the address of z as its argument.

However, the program fragment actually does something quite different. The reason is the rule that an else is always associated with the closest unmatched if inside the same pair of braces. If we were to indent this fragment the way it is actually executed, it would look like this:

```
if (x == 0) {
        if (y == 0)
                error();
        else {
                z = x + y;
                f(&z);
        }
}
```

In other words, nothing at all will happen if $x\neq0$. To get the effect implied by the indentation of the original example, write:

```
if (x == 0) {
        if (y == 0)
                error();
} else {
        z = x + y;
        f(&z);
}
```

The else here is associated with the first if, even though the second if is closer, because the second one is now enclosed in braces.

Some programming languages use explicit closing delimiters for if statements. For example, the example above would look like this in Algol 68:

```
if x = 0
then      if y = 0
          then error
          fi
else      z := x + y;
          f(z)
fi
```

Requiring closing delimiters this way completely avoids the dangling else problem, at the cost of making programs slightly longer. Some C users have tried to obtain a similar effect through macros:

```
#define IF        {if(
#define THEN      ) {
#define ELSE      } else {
#define FI        }}
```

This would allow the last C example above to be written this way:

```
IF x == 0
THEN      IF y == 0
          THEN      error();
          FI
ELSE      z = x + y;
          f(&z);
FI
```

C users not steeped in Algol 68 find this code hard to read; this solution may be worse than the problem.

Exercise 2-1. C permits an extra comma in an initializer list:

```
int days[] = { 31, 28, 31, 30, 31, 30,
               31, 31, 30, 31, 30, 31, };
```

Why is this useful? □

Exercise 2-2. We have seen several problems caused by the fact that C statements end with semicolons. While it is too late to change that now, it is fun to speculate about other ways of separating statements. How do other languages do it? Do these methods have their own pitfalls? □

CHAPTER 3: **SEMANTIC PITFALLS**

A sentence can be perfectly spelled and written with impeccable grammar and still have an ambiguous or unintentional meaning. This chapter looks at ways of writing programs that look like they mean one thing but actually mean something quite different.

It also discusses contexts in which things that look reasonable on the surface actually give undefined results in all C implementations. Things that might work on some implementations but not others are mentioned in Chapter 7, which looks at portability problems.

3.1 Pointers and arrays

The C notions of pointers and arrays are inseparably joined, to the extent that it is impossible to understand one thoroughly without also understanding the other. Moreover, C treats some aspects of these notions differently from any other well-known language.

Two things stand out about C arrays:

1. C has only one-dimensional arrays, and the size of an array must be fixed as a constant at compilation time. However, an element of an array may be an object of any type, including another array; this makes it possible to simulate multi-dimensional arrays fairly easily.

2. Only two things can be done to an array: determine its size and obtain a pointer to element 0 of the array. *All* other array operations are actually done with pointers, even if they are written with what look like subscripts. That is, every subscript operation is equivalent to a pointer operation, so it is possible to define the behavior of subscripts entirely in terms of the behavior of pointers.

Once these two points and all their implications are thoroughly understood, C array operations become much easier. Until then, they can be a rich source of confusion. In particular, it is important to be able to think about array operations and their corresponding pointer operations interchangeably. Indexing is built into most other languages; in C it is defined in terms of pointer arithmetic.

On the way to understanding how arrays work, we must understand how to declare them. For example,

```
int a[3];
```

says that a is an array of three int elements. Similarly,

```
struct {
        int p[4];
        double x;
} b[17];
```

says that b is an array of 17 elements, each of which is a structure containing an array (named p) of four int elements and a double value (named x).

Now consider

```
int calendar[12][31];
```

This says that calendar is an array of 12 arrays of 31 int elements each (not an array of 31 arrays of 12 int elements each), so that sizeof(calendar) is 372 (31×12) times sizeof(int).

If the name calendar is used in just about any context other than as the operand of sizeof, it is converted to a pointer to the initial element of calendar. To understand what this means, we must first understand some details about pointers.

Every pointer is a pointer *to some type*. For instance, if we write

```
int *ip;
```

we have said that ip is a pointer to an int. If we now say

```
int i;
```

we can assign the address of i to ip by saying

```
ip = &i;
```

and then we can change the value of i by assigning to *ip:

```
*ip = 17;
```

If a pointer happens to point to an element of an array, we can add 1 to that pointer to obtain a pointer to the next element of that array. Similarly, we can subtract 1 from the pointer to obtain a pointer to the previous element of that array, and so on for other integers.

This implies that adding an integer to a pointer is generally different from adding that integer to the bit representation of that pointer! If `ip` points to an integer, `ip+1` points to the next integer in the machine's memory, which, for most modern computers, is not the next memory location.

We can also subtract one pointer from another, provided that both of them point to elements of the same array.

This makes good sense. If we have written

```
int *q = p + i;
```

then we should be able to obtain `i` by writing `q-p`. Notice that if `p` and `q` don't point to elements of the same array, there is no way to guarantee even that the distance between `p` and `q` is an integral multiple of an array element!

We have already defined `a` as an array of three `int` values. If we use the name of an array where a pointer is appropriate, that name is taken to mean a pointer to element 0 of that array. Thus if we write

```
p = a;
```

we will set `p` to the address of element 0 of `a`. Notice that we did not say

```
p = &a;
```

That is illegal in ANSI C because `&a` is a pointer to an array but `p` is a pointer to an `int`. In most earlier versions of C, there is no notion of the address of an array — `&a` is either illegal or equivalent to `a`.

Now that `p` points to element 0 of `a`, `p+1` points to element 1, `p+2` to element 2, and so on. We can therefore make `p` point to element 1 by saying

```
p = p + 1;
```

which, of course, is equivalent to saying

```
p++;
```

The name `a` refers to the address of element 0 of `a` in every context but one: when `a` is used as an argument to the `sizeof` operator. There, `sizeof(a)` does what one would reasonably expect: it yields the size of the entire array `a` and not the size of a pointer to one of its elements!

One implication of all this is that it is possible to write `*a` as a reference to element 0 of `a`:

```
*a = 84;
```

sets element 0 of `a` to 84. In a similar vein, `*(a+1)` refers to element 1 of `a`, and so on. In general, it is possible to refer to element `i` of `a` by writing `*(a+i)`; this notion is so common that it is abbreviated as `a[i]`.

It is precisely this idea that is so hard for new C programmers to understand. In fact, since a+i and i+a mean the same thing, a[i] and i[a] *also* mean the same thing. The latter usage is definitely not recommended, although some assembly language programmers may find it familiar.

We can now think about "two-dimensional arrays," which, as we have already seen, are really arrays of arrays. While it is not hard to write programs that manipulate one-dimensional arrays purely in terms of pointers, the notational convenience of subscripts becomes nearly essential for two-dimensional arrays. Moreover, using only pointers to manipulate two-dimensional arrays leads us into some of the darker corners of the language, where compiler bugs are likely to lurk.

Consider again the declarations

```
int calendar[12][31];
int *p;
int i;
```

and ask yourself what might be the meaning of calendar[4]?

Since calendar is an array of 12 arrays of 31 int elements each, calendar[4] is simply element 4 of that array. Thus calendar[4] is one of the 12 arrays of 31 int elements in calendar and behaves *exactly* that way. So, for instance, sizeof(calendar[4]) is 31 times the size of an int, and the effect of saying

```
p = calendar[4];
```

is to make p point to element 0 of the array calendar[4].

If calendar[4] is an array, we should be able to subscript it and say

```
i = calendar[4][7];
```

and indeed we can. Again, this statement is precisely equivalent to saying

```
i = *(calendar[4] + 7);
```

which in turn is equivalent to

```
i = *(*(calendar+4) + 7);
```

Here the bracket notation is clearly more convenient.

Now look at

```
p = calendar;
```

This statement is illegal because calendar is an array of arrays; using the name calendar in this context therefore converts it to a pointer to an array. Since p is a pointer to an int, we are trying to assign a pointer of one type to a pointer of another type.

Apparently, we need a way to declare a pointer to an array. After wading through Chapter 2, it should not be too hard to construct it:

```
int (*ap)[31];
```

In effect, we are saying here that *ap is an array of 31 int elements, so ap is a pointer to such an array. We can therefore write

```
int calendar[12][31];
int (*monthp)[31];
monthp = calendar;
```

and monthp will then point to the first of the 12 31-element arrays that are the elements of calendar.

Suppose a new year is beginning and we want to clear the calendar. This is easy to do with subscripts:

```
int month;
for (month = 0; month < 12; month++) {
        int day;
        for (day = 0; day < 31; day++)
                calendar[month][day] = 0;
}
```

What is happening here in terms of pointers? It is easy enough to treat

```
calendar[month][day] = 0;
```

as

```
*(*(calendar + month) + day) = 0;
```

but what is really involved?

If monthp points to an array of 31 int values, it is possible to step monthp through calendar just as with any other pointer:

```
int (*monthp)[31];
for (monthp = calendar; monthp < &calendar[12]; monthp++)
        /* deal with a month */
```

Similarly, it is possible to deal with the elements of one of the arrays pointed to by monthp just like any other array:

```
int (*monthp)[31];
for(monthp = calendar; monthp<&calendar[12]; monthp++){
        int *dayp;
        for(dayp = *monthp; dayp<&(*monthp)[31]; dayp++)
                *dayp = 0;
}
```

At this point we have walked far enough out on the ice that we had better turn back before falling through; although this last example is valid ANSI C, I had trouble finding a compiler that would accept it. The point of this excursion has been to illustrate the unique relationship in C between arrays and pointers, with the aim of shedding more light on both.

3.2   Pointers are not arrays

A character string constant in C represents the address of an area of memory that holds the characters in the constant, followed by a null character ('\0'). Because the language prescribes null terminators for string constants, C programmers usually use that convention for other strings as well.

Suppose we have two such strings s and t, and we want to concatenate them into a single string r. To do this, we have the usual library functions strcpy and strcat. The following obvious method doesn't work:

```
char *r;
strcpy(r, s);
strcat(r, t);
```

The reason it doesn't work is that r doesn't point anywhere. Moreover, in order to make r point somewhere, it must have a place to point; that memory must be allocated somehow.

Let's try again, allocating some memory for r:

```
char r[100];
strcpy(r, s);
strcat(r, t);
```

This now works as long as the strings pointed to by s and t aren't too big. Unfortunately, C requires us to state the size of an array as a constant, so there is no way to be certain that r will be big enough. However, most C implementations have a library function called malloc that takes a number and allocates enough memory for that many characters. There is also usually a function called strlen that tells how many characters are in a string. It might seem, therefore, that we could write:

```
char *r, *malloc();
r = malloc(strlen(s) + strlen(t));
strcpy(r, s);
strcat(r, t);
```

This example, however, fails for three reasons. First, malloc might be unable to provide the requested memory, an event that it signals by returning a null pointer.

Second, it is important to remember to free the memory allocated for r when done with it. Because the previous program declared r as a local variable, r was freed automatically. The revised program allocates memory explicitly and must therefore free it explicitly.

Third, and most important, is that the call to malloc doesn't allocate quite enough memory. Recall the convention that a string is terminated by a null character. The strlen function returns the number of characters in the argument string, *excluding* the null character at the end. Therefore, if strlen(s) is *n,* s really requires *n+1* characters to contain it. We must thus allocate one extra character for r. After doing this and checking that malloc worked, we get:

```
char *r, *malloc();
r = malloc(strlen(s) + strlen(t) + 1);
if (!r) {
        complain();
        exit(1);
}
strcpy(r, s);
strcat(r, t);

/* some time later */
free(r);
```

3.3   Array declarations as parameters

There is no way to pass an array to a function directly. Using an array name as an argument immediately converts it to a pointer to the initial element of the array. For example, writing:

```
char hello[] = "hello";
```

declares hello as an array of characters. Passing that array to a function:

```
printf("%s\n", hello);
```

is precisely equivalent to passing the address of its initial character:

```
printf("%s\n", &hello[0]);
```

Thus it is never meaningful to use an array as a function parameter. For this reason, C automatically converts an array parameter declaration to the corresponding pointer declaration. In other words, writing

```
int
strlen(char s[])
{
        /* stuff */
}
```

is precisely equivalent to writing

```
strlen(char *s)
{
        /* stuff */
}
```

C programmers often suppose, incorrectly, that this automatic conversion applies in other contexts as well. Section 4.5 (page 63) discusses one particularly common trouble spot in more detail:

```
extern char *hello;
```

is definitely *not* the same as

```
extern char hello[];
```

If a pointer parameter does not represent an array, it is misleading, although technically correct, to use the array notation. What about pointer parameters that do represent arrays? One common example is the second argument to main:

```
main(int argc, char *argv[])
{
        /* stuff */
}
```

This is equivalent to

```
main(int argc, char **argv)
{
        /* stuff */
}
```

but the former example emphasizes the idea that argv is a pointer to the initial element of an array of character pointers. Because these two notations are equivalent, you can choose whichever expresses your intent most clearly.

3.4   Eschew synecdoche

A synecdoche (sin-ECK-duh-key) is a literary device, somewhat like a simile or a metaphor, in which, according to the *Oxford English Dictionary*, "a more comprehensive term is used for a less comprehensive or vice versa; as whole for part or part for whole, genus for species or species for genus, etc."

This exactly describes the common C pitfall of confusing a pointer with the data to which it points. This is most common for character strings. For instance:

```
char *p, *q;
p = "xyz";
```

It is important to understand that while it is sometimes useful to think of the value of p as the string xyz after the assignment, this is not really true. Instead, the value of p is a *pointer* to the 0th element of an array of four characters, whose values are 'x', 'y', 'z', and '\0'. Thus, if we now execute

```
q = p;
```

p and q are now two pointers to the same part of memory. The characters in that memory did not get copied by the assignment. The situation now looks like this:

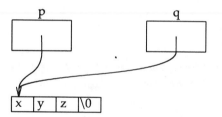

The thing to remember is that *copying a pointer does not copy the thing it addresses.*

Thus, if after this we were to execute

```
q[1] = 'Y';
```

q would point to memory containing the string xYz. So would p, because p and q point to the same memory.

3.5 Null pointers are not null strings

The result of converting an integer to a pointer is implementation-dependent, with one important exception. That exception is the constant 0, which is guaranteed to be converted to a pointer that is unequal to any valid pointer. For documentation, this value is often given symbolically:

```
#define NULL 0
```

but the effect is the same. The important thing to remember about 0 when used as a pointer is that *it must never be dereferenced*. In other words, when you have assigned 0 to a pointer variable, you must not ask what is in the memory it addresses. It is valid to write:

```
if (p == (char *) 0) ...
```

but it is not valid to write:

```
if (strcmp(p, (char *) 0) == 0) ...
```

because `strcmp` always looks at the memory addressed by its arguments.

If `p` is a null pointer, even the effects of

```
printf(p);
```

and

```
printf("%s", p);
```

are undefined. Moreover, statements like these may have different effects on different machines. Section 7.6 (page 91) says more about this.

3.6   Counting and asymmetric bounds

If an array has 10 elements, what are the permissible values of its subscripts?

Different languages answer this question differently. Fortran, PL/I, and Snobol4, for example, start subscripts from 1 but allow the programmer to specify a different origin. Algol and Pascal have no default: the programmer must give explicit lower and upper bounds for every array. In standard Basic, declaring an array with 10 elements really allocates 11: the subscripts range from 0 to 10 inclusive!

In C, subscripts run from 0 through 9. A 10-element array has a 0th element but no 10th element. A C array with n elements does not have an element with a subscript of n, as the elements are numbered from 0 through n−1. Because of this, programmers coming from other languages must be especially careful when using arrays.

For instance, let's look at the example mentioned in Section 0.0 (page 2) more closely:

```
int i, a[10];
for (i=1; i<=10; i++)
        a[i] = 0;
```

This example, intended to set the elements of a to zero, has an unexpected side effect. Because the comparison in the `for` statement is `i<=10` instead of `i<10`, the nonexistent element number 10 of a is set to zero, thus clobbering the word that follows a in memory. If this program is run on a compiler that allocates memory for variables at decreasing addresses, the word after a turns out to be i. Setting i to zero makes the loop into an infinite loop.

Although C arrays can trouble the neophyte, their particular design is actually one of the language's greatest strengths. Appreciating this requires some explanation.

Among common programming errors, the hardest to find are usually *fencepost errors*, also called *off-by-one errors*. The problem given in exercise 0.2 (page 3) gives fencepost errors their name; it asks how many fenceposts 10 feet apart it takes to support 100 feet of fence. The "obvious" answer is to divide 100 by 10 to get 10, but of course this is wrong: the right answer is 11.

Perhaps the easiest way to see this is to note that it takes two fenceposts to support 10 feet of fence: one at each end. Another way to view the problem is to realize that each segment has a post at its *left*. This accounts for all but one of the posts: the one at the *right* of the rightmost segment.

These two ways of solving this problem suggest two general principles for avoiding fencepost errors:

1. Extrapolate from a trivial case.

2. Count carefully.

With all this in mind, let's look at counting ranges of integers. For instance, how many integers x are there with $x \geqslant 16$ and $x \leqslant 37$? That is, how many elements are in the sequence 16, 17, ..., 37? It is obvious that the answer is very close to $37-16$, or 21, but is it 20, 21, or 22?

The problem would be trivial if the upper and lower bounds were the same: there is obviously one integer x with $x \geqslant 16$ and $x \leqslant 16$, namely 16. So when the upper and lower bounds match, there is one element in the sequence.

Call the lower bound l and the upper bound h. Then by saying "the upper and lower bounds match" we are saying that $l=h$, or that $h-l=0$. Thus we see that the number of elements in the sequence is $h-l+1$, which, for this example, is 22.

It is the "+1" in $h-l+1$ that is the source of so many fencepost errors. It is so tempting to assume that a substring of a string that starts at the 16th character and extends through the 37th character is 21 characters long. And this suggests a question: might there be some programming technique that makes these errors less likely?

There is, and a single rule covers it: *Express a range by the first element of the range and the first element beyond it.* In other words, instead of talking about values of x with $x \geqslant 16$ and $x \leqslant 37$, talk instead about values with $x \geqslant 16$ and $x < 38$. Use *inclusive* lower bounds and *exclusive* upper bounds. This asymmetry may look mathematically ugly, but it can simplify programming surprisingly:

1. The size of a range is the difference between the bounds. 38−16 is 22, the number of elements contained between the asymmetric bounds 16 and 38.

2. The bounds are equal when the range is empty. This follows immediately from (1).

3. The upper bound is never less than the lower bound, not even when the range is empty.

Asymmetric bounds are most convenient to program in a language like C in which arrays start from zero: the exclusive upper bound of such an array is equal to the number of elements! Thus when we define a C array with 10 elements, 0 is the inclusive lower bound and 10 the exclusive upper bound for the subscripts of that array. It is for that reason that we write

```
int a[10], i;
for (i = 0; i < 10; i++)
        a[i] = 0;
```

instead of

```
int a[10], i;
for (i = 0; i <= 9; i++)
        a[i] = 0;
```

If C had an Algol- or Pascal-style `for` statement, that would introduce a pitfall: what would this mean?

```
for (i = 0 to 10)
        a[i] = 0;
```

If 10 were an inclusive bound, i would take on 11 values, not 10; if 10 were an exclusive bound, it would surprise programmers raised on other languages.

Another way to think of asymmetric bounds is to realize that they represent the *first occupied* and *first free* elements of some sequence:

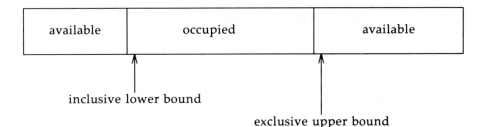

This way of looking at things is particularly useful when dealing with buffers of various sorts. For example, consider a function whose job it is to collect input of irregular length into blocks of N characters and write out a buffer-load when it becomes full. The declaration for the buffer might look something like this:

```
#define N 1024
static char buffer[N];
```

with a pointer variable to mark the current place in the buffer:

```
static char *bufptr;
```

What significance shall we attach to `bufptr`? It may be tempting to establish that `bufptr` always points at the last occupied character in the buffer, but our preference for asymmetric bounds causes us to make `bufptr` represent the first free character in the buffer.

With that convention, we put a character c into the buffer by writing

```
*bufptr++ = c;
```

and when we are done, `bufptr` again points at the first free character.

Our observations about asymmetric bounds show us that the buffer will be empty when `bufptr` and `&buffer[0]` are equal, so we initially say the buffer is empty by writing

```
bufptr = &buffer[0];
```

or, more simply,

```
bufptr = buffer;
```

The number of characters in the buffer at any time is just `bufptr-buffer`, so we can test if the buffer is completely full by seeing if this expression is equal to N. Since the buffer is completely full when `bufptr-buffer` and N are equal, the number of characters available in the buffer must therefore be `N-(bufptr-buffer)`.

With these preliminary observations out of the way, we are ready to write our program, which we will call `bufwrite`. Its arguments are a pointer to the first character to be written and a count of the number of characters to write. We assume we can call a function `flushbuffer` to write out the contents of the buffer and that `flushbuffer` will reset `bufptr` to the beginning of the buffer.

```
void
bufwrite(char *p, int n)
{
        while (--n >= 0) {
                if (bufptr == &buffer[N])
                        flushbuffer();
                *bufptr++ = *p++;
        }
}
```

Iterating the expression `--n>=0` is one way of doing something n times. To see this, look at a trivial case such as $n=1$.† Since the loop is executed n times and each iteration fetches a single character from the input buffer, we know we will handle every input character and no more.

Note the comparison with `&buffer[N]`: there is no such element! Elements of `buffer` are numbered from 0 to N-1. We have written

```
        if (bufptr == &buffer[N])
```

instead of the effectively equivalent

```
        if (bufptr > &buffer[N-1])
```

because we are sticking to our principles about asymmetric bounds: we want to compare `bufptr` to the address of the first character *following* the buffer, and `&bufptr[N]` is precisely that address. But how can it make sense to refer to an element that doesn't exist?

Fortunately we do not have to refer to this element, merely to its address, and that address *does* exist in every C implementation we have encountered. Moreover, ANSI C explicitly permits this usage: the address of the nonexistent element just past the end of an array may be taken and used for assignment and comparison purposes. Of course it is illegal actually to *refer* to that element!

Our program works as written, but we can speed it up. Optimization is generally beyond the scope of this book, but this particular case is worth examining for its counting aspects.

---

† On most C implementations, `--n>=0` is likely to be at least as fast as the equivalent `n-->0` and faster on some. The first expression subtracts one from n and compares the result to zero. The second saves n, subtracts one from n, and then compares the saved value to zero. Some compilers will be clever enough to realize this can be done more efficiently than written, but why count on it?

Most of this program's overhead is there because each iteration of the loop tests *two* things: whether the loop count has been exhausted and whether the buffer is full. This in turn is the result of moving one character at a time into the buffer.

Let us assume that we have a way of moving k characters at a time. Most C implementations (and all correct ANSI C implementations) have a function called memcpy that does this; this function is often implemented in assembly language for speed. The function is easy to write for those implementations that don't have it:

```
void
memcpy(char *dest, const char *source, int k)
{
        while (--k >= 0)
                *dest++ = *source++;
}
```

We can make bufwrite take advantage of memcpy by moving characters into the buffer in chunks instead of one at a time. Each iteration of the loop will therefore flush the buffer if needed, calculate how many characters to move, move them, and update counters appropriately:

```
void
bufwrite(char *p, int n)
{
        while (n > 0) {
                int k, rem;
                if (bufptr == &buffer[N])
                        flushbuffer();
                rem = N - (bufptr - buffer);
                k = n > rem? rem: n;
                memcpy(bufptr, p, k);
                bufptr += k;
                p += k;
                n -= k;
        }
}
```

Many programmers hesitate to write this sort of program for fear of getting it wrong. Others are fearless — and do get it wrong. Indeed, this sort of thing is tricky and should not be attempted without good reason. But if there is a good reason, it is important to understand how to do it. And by checking trivial cases and counting carefully, it is possible to be confident of getting it right.

At entry to the loop, n is the number of characters to be placed in the buffer. Thus it is clearly right to continue as long as n>0. Each time through the loop, we are going to transfer some number k of characters into the buffer. The last four statements manage that transfer by (1) copying k characters starting at the first free character in the buffer, (2) advancing the first free location by k characters, (3) advancing the input pointer by k characters, and (4) decreasing the number of characters to write by k. It is easy to see that these statements do the right thing.

The beginning of the loop retains the test from the previous version: if the buffer is full, flush it (and reset bufptr). Thus after this test, there is guaranteed to be some room in the buffer.

The only hard part, then, is determining k, which should be the largest number of characters that can safely fit into the buffer. That value is the smaller of two quantities: the number of characters remaining in the input (n) and the number of free characters remaining in the buffer (which we will place in rem).

There are two ways to calculate rem. Our example shows one: the number of characters presently available is the number of characters occupied (bufptr-buffer) subtracted from the total number of characters in the buffer (N), or N-(bufptr-buffer).

The other way is to view the *empty* part of the buffer as an interval and calculate its size directly. If we do this, then bufptr represents the beginning of the interval and buffer+N (equivalent to &buffer[N]) represents (one character past) the end. This viewpoint thus says that there are (buffer+N)-bufptr characters still available in the buffer. A little reflection shows that

```
    (buffer+N)-bufptr
```

and

```
    N-(bufptr-buffer)
```

are equivalent.

Here is another counting example: given a program that generates integers in some sequence, print those integers in columns. More precisely, the output should consist of some number of pages, each of which contains NCOLS columns of NROWS elements each. Consecutive values are obtained by reading down the columns, not across the rows.

We will make several simplifying assumptions to concentrate on the counting aspects of the problem. First, we assume that our program will be expressed as a pair of functions called print and flush. Some other program is responsible for deciding what values to print; that program will designate values to be printed by calling print each time a new value is known and flush once after the last value has been generated. Second, we will assume that we can use three functions to do our printing: printnum prints a single value at the current place on the page,

`printnl` begins a new line, and `printpage` begins a new page. Every
line must end with a call to `printnl`, even the last one on a page. These
functions fill each output line from left to right; once a line has been
printed there is no way to back up or change it.

The first thing to realize about this problem is that we cannot get by
without a buffer of some sort: we do not know the contents of the first
element of the second column until after we have seen all the elements
of the first column, but we must print the entire first *row* before we can
even print the second element of the first column!

How large must this buffer be? At first glance it seems to have to be
big enough to contain an entire page full of numbers, but deeper reflection argues that this is not so: we can always print an element of the *last*
column as soon as we have it, because by definition we have all the
information we need to do so. Thus our buffer can omit the last column:

```
#define BUFSIZE (NROWS*(NCOLS-1))
static int buffer[BUFSIZE];
```

We declare the buffer `static` to forestall the possibility of its being
accessed by some other part of this program. Section 4.3 (page 56) says
more about `static` declarations.

Our strategy for `print` is going to be roughly as follows: put the
value in the buffer unless the buffer is already full, in which case we
must print the entire line containing this value. When printing that line
empties the buffer, we have ended a page.

Note that the values do not come out of the buffer in the same
sequence they went in: we receive values by columns but must print
them by rows. That leaves open the question of whether rows or
columns should be adjacent in the buffer; we arbitrarily choose to make
the elements of a column adjacent. That means that incoming elements
will simply go into consecutive locations in the buffer, but they will
come out in a more complicated fashion. To keep track of elements on
their way into the buffer, therefore, a simple pointer will suffice. We initialize it to point at the first element in the buffer:

```
static int *bufptr = buffer;
```

At this point we have a partial idea about the structure of `print`. It takes
an integer argument and puts it into the buffer if the buffer has room.
Otherwise it does something mysterious. Let's write down what we have
so far:

```
void
print(int n)
{
        if (bufptr == &buffer[BUFSIZE]) {
                /* do something mysterious */
        } else
                *bufptr++ = n;
}
```

This "something mysterious" is to print all the elements in the current
row, increment the notion of the current row, and start a new page if
we've printed all the rows on the current one. For this, we evidently
need to remember the row number; we'll do that with a (local) static
variable row.

How do we print all the elements in the current row? This looks
messy at first, but is actually very easy if looked at properly. We know
that the first element in row number row is just buffer[row], and that
element buffer[row] exists because we wouldn't be here if the first
column were not completely full. We also know that adjacent elements
in a row are separated by NROWS elements. Finally, we know that
bufptr points just beyond the last occupied element in the buffer. Thus
we can print all the elements in the buffer that are in the current row
with the following loop:

```
int *p;
for (p = buffer+row; p < bufptr; p += NROWS)
        printnum(*p);
```

Here we write buffer+row instead of &buffer[row] for compactness.

The rest of the "something mysterious" is simple: write the current
number, end the row, and start a new page if we've just printed the last
row:

```
printnum(n);
printnl();
if (++row == NROWS) {
        printpage();
        row = 0;
        bufptr = buffer;
}
```

Thus the entire print function looks like this:

```
void
print(int n)
{
        if (bufptr == &buffer[BUFSIZE]) {
                static int row = 0;
                int *p;
                for (p = buffer+row; p < bufptr;
                                p += NROWS)
                        printnum(*p);
                printnum(n);
                printnl();
                if (++row == NROWS) {
                        printpage();
                        row = 0;
                        bufptr = buffer;
                }
        } else
                *bufptr++ = n;

}
```

Now we are almost done: we just need to write flush, whose job is to print the partial page that remains in the buffer. This is done by using what is essentially the same inner loop as printnum, repeating it for each row:

```
void
flush()
{
        int row;
        for (row = 0; row < NROWS; row++) {
                int *p;
                for (p = buffer+row; p < bufptr;
                                p += NROWS)
                        printnum(*p);
                printnl();
        }
        printpage();
}
```

This version of flush is a little literal-minded: if the last page consists only of a single (partial) column, it is padded out to its full length with blank lines. In fact, if the last page is empty, it will be printed anyway, consisting entirely of blank lines. While this is technically within the problem definition, aesthetic considerations suggest that we should stop printing as soon as we have run out of things to print. We do this by calculating how many items are in the buffer. If there is nothing to print, we don't start a new page, either:

```
void
flush()
{
        int row;
        int k = bufptr - buffer;
        if (k > NROWS)
                k = NROWS;
        if (k > 0) {
                for (row = 0; row < k; row++) {
                        int *p;
                        for (p = buffer+row; p < bufptr;
                                        p += NROWS)
                                printnum(*p);
                        printnl();
                }
                printpage();
        }
}
```

3.7   Order of evaluation

Section 2.2 (page 17) discussed precedence. Order of evaluation is a different matter entirely. Precedence is what says that the expression

```
a + b * c
```

is interpreted as

```
a + (b * c)
```

and not as

```
(a + b) * c
```

Order of evaluation is what guarantees that

```
if (count != 0 && sum/count < smallaverage)
        printf ("average < %g\n", smallaverage);
```

will not cause a "divide by zero" error even if count is zero.

Some C operators always evaluate their operands in a known, specified order. Others don't. Consider, for instance, the following expression:

```
a < b && c < d
```

The language definition states that a<b will be evaluated first. If a is indeed less than b, c<d must then be evaluated to determine the value of the whole expression. On the other hand, if a is greater than or equal to b, then c<d is not evaluated at all.

To evaluate a<b, on the other hand, the compiler may evaluate either a or b first. On some machines, it may even evaluate them in parallel.

Only the four C operators &&, ¦¦, ?:, and , specify an order of evaluation. && and ¦¦ evaluate the left operand first, and the right operand only if necessary. The ?: operator takes three operands: a?b:c evaluates a first, and then evaluates either b or c, depending on the value of a. The , operator evaluates its left operand and discards its value, then evaluates its right operand.†

All other C operators evaluate their operands in undefined order. In particular, the assignment operators do not make any guarantees about evaluation order.

The && and ¦¦ operators are important for ensuring that tests are applied in the right sequence. For instance, in

```
if (y != 0 && x/y > tolerance)
        complain();
```

it is essential to evaluate x/y only if y is nonzero.

The following way of copying the first n elements of array x to array y is incorrect because it assumes too much about order of evaluation:

```
i = 0;
while (i < n)
        y[i] = x[i++];
```

The trouble is that there is no guarantee that the address of y[i] will be evaluated before i is incremented. On some implementations, it will; on others, it won't. This similar version fails for the same reason:

```
i = 0;
while (i < n)
        y[i++] = x[i];
```

On the other hand, this one will work fine:

```
i = 0;
while (i < n) {
        y[i] = x[i];
        i++;
}
```

This can, of course, be abbreviated:

---

† Commas that separate function arguments are not comma operators. For example, x and y are fetched in undefined order in f(x,y), but not in g((x,y)). In the latter example, g has one argument. The value of that argument is determined by evaluating x, discarding its value, and then evaluating y.

```
for (i = 0; i < n; i++)
        y[i] = x[i];
```

3.8   The &&, ¦¦, and ! operators

C has two classes of logical operators that are *sometimes* interchangeable: the bitwise operators &, ¦, and ~, and the logical operators &&, ¦¦, and !. A programmer who substitutes one of these operators for the corresponding operator from the other class may be in for a surprise: the program may appear to work correctly after such an interchange but may actually be working only by coincidence.

The &, ¦, and ~ operators treat their operands as a sequence of bits and work on each bit separately. For example, 10&12 is 8 (1000 binary), because & looks at the binary representations of 10 (1010 binary) and 12 (1100 binary) and produces a result that has a bit turned on for each bit that is on in the same position in both operands. Similarly, 10¦12 is 14 (1110 binary) and ~10 is −11 (11...110101 binary), at least on a 2's complement machine.

The &&, ¦¦, and ! operators, on the other hand, treat their arguments as if they are either "true" or "false," with the convention that 0 represents "false" and any other value represents "true." These operators return 1 for "true" and 0 for "false," they never return anything but 1 or 0, and the && and ¦¦ operators do not even evaluate their right-hand operands if their results can be determined from their left-hand operands.

Thus !10 is 0 because 10 is nonzero, 10&&12 is 1 because both 10 and 12 are nonzero, and 10¦¦12 is also 1 because 10 is nonzero. Moreover, 12 is not even evaluated in the latter expression, nor is f() in 10¦¦f().

Consider the following program fragment to look for a particular element in a table:

```
i = 0;
while (i < tabsize && tab[i] != x)
        i++;
```

The idea behind this loop is that if i is equal to tabsize when the loop terminates, then the element sought was not found. Otherwise, i contains the element's index. Note the use of asymmetric bounds in this loop.

Suppose that the && were inadvertently replaced by &:

```
i = 0;
while (i < tabsize & tab[i] != x)
      i++;
```

Then the loop would probably still appear to work, but would do so only because of two lucky breaks.

The first is that both comparisons in this example are of a kind that yield 0 if the condition is false and 1 if the condition is true. As long as x and y are both 1 or 0, x&y and x&&y will always have the same value. However, if one of the comparisons were to be replaced by one that uses some nonzero value other than 1 to represent "true," then the loop would stop working.

The second lucky break is that looking just one element off the end of an array is usually harmless, provided that the program doesn't change that element. The modified program looks past the end of the array because &, unlike &&, must always evaluate both of its operands. Thus in the last iteration of the loop, the value of tab[i] will be fetched even though i is equal to tabsize. If tabsize is the number of elements in tab, this will fetch a nonexistent element of tab.

Recall that in Section 3.6 (page 40) we said that it was legal to take the address of the element one past the end of an array. Here we are actually trying to access the element itself; the effect of that is undefined and very few C implementations will diagnose the error.

3.9   Integer overflow

C has two kinds of integer arithmetic: signed and unsigned. There is no such thing as overflow in unsigned arithmetic: all unsigned operations are done modulo 2^n, where n is the number of bits in the result. If one operand of an arithmetic operator is signed and the other unsigned, the signed operand is converted to unsigned and overflow is still impossible. But overflow can occur if both operands are signed; the result of an overflow is *undefined*. It is not safe to assume anything about the result of an operation that overflows.

Suppose, for example, that a and b are two int variables known to be nonnegative and you want to test whether a+b might overflow. One obvious way to do it is:

```
if (a + b < 0)
        complain();
```

This does not work. Once a+b has overflowed, all bets are off as to what the result will be. For example, on some machines, an addition operation sets an internal register to one of four states: positive, negative, zero, or overflow. On such a machine, the compiler would have every right to implement the example given above by adding a and b and checking whether this internal register was in negative state afterwards. If the operation overflowed, the register would be in overflow state, and the test would fail.

One correct way of doing this is to convert a and b to unsigned:

```
if ((unsigned) a + (unsigned) b > INT_MAX)
        complain();
```

Here, INT_MAX is a defined constant that represents the largest possible int value. ANSI C defines INT_MAX in <limits.h>; you may have to define it yourself on other implementations.

Another possibility doesn't involve unsigned arithmetic at all:

```
if (a > INT_MAX - b)
        complain();
```

3.10   Returning a value from main

The simplest possible C program:

```
main()
{
}
```

contains a subtle error. Like any other function, main is presumed to yield an int value if no other return type is declared for it. But no return value is given in this program.

This generally causes no harm. An int function that fails to return a value usually implicitly returns some garbage integer. As long as no one uses this value, it doesn't matter.

However, there are some contexts in which the value returned from main does matter. Many C implementations use the value returned from main to tell the operating system whether the program succeeded or failed. Typically, a 0 return indicates success and any other value indicates failure. A program that doesn't return any value from main thus probably appears to have failed. This may cause surprising results when used with things like software administration systems that care about whether programs fail after they have invoked them.

Strictly speaking, then, our minimal C program should be written this way:

```
main()
{
        return 0;
}
```

or this way:

```
main()
{
        exit(0);
}
```

and the classic "hello world" program should look like this:

```
#include <stdio.h>

main()
{
        printf("Hello world\n");
        return 0;
}
```

Exercise 3-1. Suppose it were illegal even to generate the address of an array element that is out of bounds. How would the bufwrite programs in Section 3.6 (page 39) look? □

Exercise 3-2. Compare the last version of flush shown in Section 3.6 (page 45) with this one:

```
void
flush()
{
        int row;
        int k = bufptr - buffer;
        if (k > NROWS)
                k = NROWS;
        for (row = 0; row < k; row++) {
                int *p;
                for (p = buffer+row; p < bufptr;
                                p += NROWS)
                        printnum(*p);
                printnl();
        }
        if (k > 0)
                printpage();
}
```

□

Exercise 3-3. Write a function to do a binary search in a sorted table of integers. Its input is a pointer to the beginning of the table, a count of the elements in the table, and a value to be sought. Its output is a pointer to the element sought or a NULL pointer if the element is not present. □

A C program may consist of several parts that are compiled separately and then bound together by a program usually called a *linker, linkage editor,* or *loader.* Because the compiler normally sees only one file at a time, it cannot detect errors whose recognition would require knowledge of several source program files at once. Moreover, the linker on many systems is beyond the control of the C implementer and thus cannot readily detect C errors either.

Some C implementations, but not all, have a program called lint that catches many of these errors. It is impossible to overemphasize the importance of using such a program if it is available.

In this chapter, we look at a typical linker, note how it deals with C programs, and draw conclusions about errors that are likely to result from the nature of linkers.

4.1 What is a linker?

An important idea in C is *separate compilation:* several programs can be compiled at different times and bound together. But the linker is separate from the C compiler and can't know too much about the details of C; how can it know how to combine C programs? Although linkers don't understand C, they do understand machine language and memory layout, and it is up to each C compiler to translate C programs into terms that make sense to the linker.

A typical linker combines several *object modules* produced by a compiler or assembler together into a single entity, sometimes called a *load module* or an *executable file*, that the operating system can execute directly. Some of those object modules are given directly as input to the linker; others are fetched on demand from a *library* of object modules containing printf and similar things.

A linker typically views an object module as containing a collection of *external objects*. Each external object represents the contents of some part of the machine's memory and is identified by an *external name*. Thus every function not declared static is an external object, as is every external variable not declared static. Some implementations make static functions and variables into external objects as well by transforming their names somehow so that they do not clash with identically named variables in other source program files.

Most linkers forbid two different external objects in a single load module to have the same name. However, several object modules to be combined into a single load module might contain identically-named external objects. One important job of a linker is to handle these name conflicts.

The simplest way to handle such a conflict is to prohibit it. This is surely correct if the external objects are functions: a program that contains two different functions with the same name should be rejected. The problem is harder, though, if the objects are variables. Different linkers handle that situation in different ways; we will see the significance of this later.

With this information, it begins to become possible to imagine how a linker works. Its input is some collection of object modules and libraries. Its output is a load module, which it builds as it reads its input. For each external object in each object module, it checks whether an object of that name already appears in the load module. If not, it adds it. If so, it deals with the conflict somehow.

In addition to external objects, object modules may contain *references* to external objects in other modules. For example, an object module resulting from a C program that calls printf will contain a reference to the printf function, which is presumably an external object in a library somewhere. As it builds the load module, the linker must keep track of these external references. When it reads an object module, it *resolves* all the references to external objects defined in that module by noting that those objects are no longer undefined.

Because linkers don't know much about C, there are many errors they cannot detect. If your implementation has a lint program, use it!

4.2 Declarations vs. definitions

The declaration

        int a;

appearing outside of any function body is called a *definition* of the external object a; it says that a is an external integer variable and also allocates storage for it. Because it doesn't specify an initial value, the value is assumed to be 0 (on systems whose linkers don't guarantee this for programs in other languages, is is up to the C compiler to utter the appropriate incantations to the linker to ensure it).

The declaration

```
int a = 7;
```

is a definition of a that includes an explicit initial value. Not only does it allocate memory for a, but it says what value that memory should have.

The declaration

```
extern int a;
```

is not a definition of a. It still says that a is an external integer variable, but by including the extern keyword, it explicitly says that the storage for a is allocated somewhere else. From the linker's viewpoint, such a declaration is a *reference* to the external object a but does not define it. Because this declaration explicitly refers to an external object, it has the same meaning even inside a function. The following function srand stores a copy of its integer argument in the external variable random_seed:

```
void
srand(int n)
{
        extern int random_seed;
        random_seed = n;
}
```

Every external object must be defined somewhere. Thus a program that includes

```
extern int a;
```

must say

```
int a;
```

somewhere else, either in the same program file or a different one.

What about a program that defines the same external variable more than once? That is, suppose

```
int a;
```

appears in each of two or more separate source program files? Or what if

```
int a = 7;
```

appears in one file and

```
int a = 9;
```

appears in another? Here systems vary. The strict rule is that every external variable must be defined *exactly once*. If each of several external definitions supplies an initial value, such as

```
int a = 7;
```

in one file and

```
int a = 5;
```

in another, most systems will reject the program. But if an external variable is defined in several files *without* an initial value, some systems will accept the program and others won't. The only way to avoid this trouble in all C implementations is to define each external variable exactly once.

4.3   Name conflicts and the `static` modifier

Two external objects with the same name are the same object, even if the programmer didn't intend it that way. Thus two separate source program files, each of which contains the definition

```
int a;
```

either represent an error (if the linker prohibits duplicate external variables) or will share a single instance of a whether they wanted to share a or not.

This is true even if one of the definitions of a is in the system library. Of course, an intelligently designed library will not define a as an external name, but it is not easy to know all the names that the library does define. Names like `read` and `write` are easy to guess, but others might not be so easy.

ANSI C makes it easier to avoid conflicting with library names by listing all the functions that might possibly cause such conflicts. Any library function that calls another library function not on the list must do so by a "hidden name." This allows a programmer to define a function called, say, `read` without worrying that `getc` will call that `read` instead of the system function. But most C implementations do not yet behave this way, so these conflicts are still a problem.

One useful tool for reducing conflicts of this sort is the `static` modifier. For example, the declaration

```
static int a;
```

means the same thing as

```
int a;
```

within a single source program file, but a is hidden from other files. Thus if there are several functions that need to share a collection of external objects, put all the functions into a single file and declare the objects they need as `static` in the same file.

This applies to functions too. If a function `f` calls a function `g`, and *only* `f` needs to be able to call `g`, we can put `f` and `g` in the same file and make `g` `static`:

```
static int
g(int x)
{
        /* stuff */
}

void f()
{
        /* more stuff */
        b = g(a);
}
```

We can have several files, each with its own function called `g`, as long as all of them, or all but one, are declared `static`. Thus a function that will be called only by other functions in the same file should always be declared as `static` to avoid inadvertent collisions.

4.4   Arguments, parameters, and return values

Every C function has a list of *parameters*, each of which is a variable that is initialized as part of calling the function. This function has one `int` parameter:

```
int
abs(int n)
{
        return n<0? -n: n;
}
```

For some functions, the list of parameters is empty:

```
void
eatline()
{
        int c;
        do c = getchar();
        while (c != EOF && c != '\n');
}
```

A function is called by presenting it with a list of *arguments*. In this example, a–b is the argument to abs:

```
if (abs(a-b) > n)
        printf("difference is out of range\n");
```

A function with an empty parameter list is called with an empty argument list:

```
eatline();
```

Every C function also has a *result type,* which is either void or the type of the result that the function yields. Result types are easier to understand than argument types, so we will discuss them first.

There is no trouble with result types if every function is defined or declared *before its first call* in every file that calls it. For example, consider a function square that squares its double argument:

```
double
square(double x)
{
        return x * x;
}
```

and a program that uses square:

```
main()
{
        printf("%g\n", square(0.3));
}
```

For this program to work, either square must be defined before main:

```
double
square(double x)
{
        return x * x;
}

main()
{
        printf("%g\n", square(0.3));
}
```

or square must be declared before main:

```
double square(double);

main()
{
        printf("%g\n", square(0.3));
}

double
square(double x)
{
        return x * x;
}
```

A function called before it is defined or declared is assumed to return int. Thus if main is split off into a file by itself:

```
main()
{
        printf("%g\n", square(0.3));
}
```

it will give incorrect results when linked with square because main assumes that square returns an int when actually square returns a double.

What if we wanted to define main and square in two separate files? There can be only one definition of square. If the call and definition are in different files, the calling file must declare square:

```
double square(double);

main()
{
        printf("%g\n", square(0.3));
}
```

The rules for matching arguments with parameters are a little more complicated. ANSI C allows the programmer to specify the types of function arguments in declarations:

```
double square(double);
```

says that square is a function that takes a double argument and returns a double result. After this declaration, square(2) is legal; the integer 2 will be converted to double as if the programmer had written square((double)2) or square(2.0).

If a function has no float, short, or char parameters, it is possible to omit the parameter types entirely from the function declaration (but not the definition). Thus even in ANSI C it is possible to declare square this way:

```
double square();
```

Doing this relies on the *caller* to supply the right number of arguments of appropriate types. *Appropriate* does not necessarily mean *equal*: float arguments are automatically converted to double and short or char arguments are converted to int. Thus the function

```
int
isvowel(char c)
{
        return c == 'a' || c == 'e' || c == 'i' ||
            c == 'o' || c == 'u';
}
```

must be declared in every other file that calls it:

```
int isvowel(char);
```

Otherwise the caller of isvowel would convert its argument to int, which would not match its parameter. If isvowel were defined this way:

```
int
isvowel(int c)
{
        return c == 'a' || c == 'e' || c == 'i' ||
            c == 'o' || c == 'u';
}
```

its callers would not need to declare it, even if calling it with a char argument.

Pre-ANSI C compilers do not all support this style of declaration. When using such compilers, it may be necessary to declare isvowel this way:

```
int isvowel();
```

and define it this way:

```
int
isvowel(c)
        char c;
{
        return c == 'a' || c == 'e' || c == 'i' ||
            c == 'o' || c == 'u';
}
```

For compatibility with prior usage, ANSI C supports this older form of declaration and definition as well. This raises a problem: if a file that calls `isvowel` cannot declare its parameter type (in order to work on older compilers), how does the compiler know the parameter is char and not int? The answer is that the two different definition forms mean different things; the last definition of `isvowel` above is essentially equivalent to this:

```
int
isvowel(int i)
{
        char c = i;
        return c == 'a' || c == 'e' || c == 'i' ||
               c == 'o' || c == 'u';
}
```

Now that we've seen some of the details of function declarations and definitions, let's look at some ways to get them wrong. The following simple program fails for two reasons:

```
main()
{
        double s;
        s = sqrt(2);
        printf("%g\n", s);
}
```

The first reason is that `sqrt` expects a `double` value as its argument and gets an `int` instead. The second is that it returns a `double` result but isn't declared that way.

One way to correct it is:

```
double sqrt(double);

main()
{
        double s;
        s = sqrt(2);
        printf("%g\n", s);
}
```

Another way, which works on pre-ANSI compilers as well, is

```
double sqrt();

main()
{
        double s;
        s = sqrt(2.0);
        printf("%g\n", s);
}
```

Best of all is

```
#include <math.h>

main()
{
        double s;
        s = sqrt(2.0);
        printf("%g\n", s);
}
```

This program does not contain any explicit knowledge of the argument or return types of sqrt: it takes that information instead from the system header file math.h. On ANSI compilers, this will even ensure that the argument 2.0 is converted to the proper type, although the example caters to older compilers by writing the argument as a double rather than an int.

Because the printf and scanf functions may be given arguments of different types at different times, they are particularly prone to problems. Here is a spectacular example:

```
#include <stdio.h>

main()
{
        int i;
        char c;
        for (i=0; i<5; i++) {
                scanf("%d", &c);
                printf("%d ", i);
        }
        printf("\n");
}
```

Ostensibly, this program reads five numbers from its standard input and writes

```
0  1  2  3  4
```

on its standard output. In fact, it doesn't always do that. On one compiler, for example, its output is

```
0 0 0 0 0 1 2 3 4
```

Why? The key is the declaration of c as a char rather than as an int. When you ask scanf to read an integer, it expects a pointer to an integer. What it gets in this case is a pointer to a character. The scanf function has no way to tell that it didn't get what it expected: it treats its input as an integer pointer and stores an integer there. Since an integer takes up more memory than a character, this steps on some of the memory near c.

Exactly what is near c is the compiler's business; in this case it turns out to be the low-order part of i. Therefore, each time a value is read for c, it resets i to zero. When the program finally reaches end of file, scanf stops trying to put new values into c, so i can be incremented normally to end the loop.

4.5 Checking external types

Suppose you have a C program divided into two files. One file contains the declaration:

```
extern int n;
```

and the other contains the definition:

```
long n;
```

In each case, the declaration is assumed to be outside the body of any function, so it has external scope.

This is not a valid C program because the same external name is declared with two different types in the two files. However, many implementations will fail to detect this error. The compiler handles each of these program files separately — they could have been compiled months apart. Thus the compiler does not know about the contents of either of the two files while it is compiling the other. The linker probably doesn't know anything about C, so it doesn't know how to compare the types of the two definitions of n.

What actually happens when this program is run? There are many possibilities:

1. The implementation is clever enough to detect the type clash. One would then expect to see a diagnostic message explaining that the type of n was given differently in two different files.

2. You are using an implementation that represents int and long values the same way internally. This is typically true of machines in which

32-bit arithmetic comes most naturally. In this case, your program will probably work as if you had said `long` (or `int`) in both declarations. This is a good example of a program that works only by coincidence.

3. The two instances of n require different amounts of storage, but they happen to share storage in such a way that the values assigned to one are valid for the other. This might happen, for example, if the linker arranged for the `int` to share storage with the low-order part of the `long` and every value stored in the `long` could fit in an `int`. This is an even better example of a program that works only by coincidence.

4. The two instances of n share storage in such a way that assigning a value to one has the effect of apparently assigning a different value to the other. In this case, the program will probably fail.

Thus the programmer is generally responsible for ensuring that all external definitions of a particular name have the same type in every object module. Moreover, "the same type" should be taken seriously. For example, consider a program with this definition:

```
char filename[] = "/etc/passwd";
```

in one file and this declaration:

```
extern char *filename;
```

in another. Although arrays and pointers are very similar in some contexts, *they are not the same.* In the first declaration, `filename` is the name of a character array. Although a statement that refers to the value of `filename` will get a pointer to the first element of that array, the type of `filename` is "character array," not "character pointer." In the second declaration, `filename` is asserted to be a pointer. These two declarations of `filename` use storage in different ways; they cannot meaningfully coexist. The first example looks like this:

while the second one looks like this:

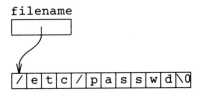

To correct this example, change either the declaration or definition of filename to match the other. Thus either say

```
char filename[] = "/etc/passwd";
```

in one file and

```
extern char filename[];
```

in the other or say

```
char *filename = "/etc/passwd";
```

in one file and

```
extern char *filename;
```

in the other.

Another easy way to get into trouble with external types is to neglect to declare the type returned by a function or to declare the wrong type. For example, recall the program from Section 4.4 (page 61)

```
main()
{
        double s;
        s = sqrt(2);
        printf("%g\n", s);
}
```

This program does not contain a declaration for sqrt; its type must therefore be inferred from the context. The rule in C is that an otherwise undeclared identifier followed by an open parenthesis is assumed to be a function that returns an integer. Therefore, the effect of this program is precisely the same as if it had been written this way:

```
extern int sqrt();

main()
{
        double s;
        s = sqrt(2);
        printf("%g\n", s);
}
```

This, of course, is wrong; sqrt returns a double, not an int. Thus the result of this program is unpredictable. In fact, it may actually appear to work on some machines! Imagine, for example, a machine that uses the same registers for integer and floating-point return values. Such a machine would take the bits it gets from sqrt and pass them on to printf without looking at them. If printf gets the right bits, it may well print the right answer. Some machines store integers and pointers in different registers; it is possible for this kind of mistake to cause failure on such a machine even if no floating-point arithmetic is involved.

4.6 Header files

One good way to avoid many problems of this sort is to adopt a simple rule: *declare each external object in one place only*. That place will usually be in a header file, which should be included by every module that uses that external object. In particular, it should be included by the module that defines the object.

For example, look again at our filename example. This might be part of a program with several modules, each of which needs to know the name of a particular file. We want to be able to change that name in every module by changing it in only one place. We do this by creating a file called, say, file.h, which contains the declaration:

```
extern char filename[];
```

Every C source file that wants to use this external object should say:

```
#include "file.h"
```

Finally, we choose one C source file to give filename its initial value. We might call it file.c:

```
#include "file.h"
char filename[] = "/etc/passwd";
```

Notice that file.c actually contains two declarations for filename: after expanding the include statement, file.c looks like this:

```
extern char filename[];
char filename[] = "/etc/passwd";
```

This is legal as long as all the declarations are consistent and at most one of the declarations is a definition.

Notice the effect of this. The type of `filename` is declared in `file.h,` so it is automatically stated correctly in every module that includes `file.h`. The `file.c` definition module includes `file.h` so the type in the definition automatically matches the type in the declaration. If all this stuff compiles, the types must be right!

Exercise 4-1. Suppose a program contains the declaration

```
long foo;
```

in one file and

```
extern short foo;
```

in another. Suppose further that assigning a small value, say 37, to the `long` version of `foo` results in giving the `short` version the value 37 as well. What likely inference follows about the hardware? What if the `short` version becomes 0 instead? □

Exercise 4-2. Here's one of the incorrect programs from Section 4.4 (page 61) after simplification:

```
#include <stdio.h>

main()
{
        printf("%g\n", sqrt(2));
}
```

On some systems, this will print

```
%g
```

Why? □

CHAPTER 5: **LIBRARY FUNCTIONS**

Every useful C program must use library functions because C does not have any input-output statements. The ANSI C standard recognizes this by defining a large collection of standard library routines that are expected to be made available by every C implementation. This collection is not complete. For example, virtually every C implementation has functions called `read` and `write` for doing "low-level" I/O, but these functions do not appear in the ANSI standard. Moreover, not all standard functions are part of every C implementation — ANSI C is too new for that.

Most library routines cause little trouble: they are straightforward enough that people seem to get them right most of the time. However, there are a few cases where some widely-used library functions behave in ways their users might not expect. In particular, programmers often seem to have trouble with the details of the `printf` family of functions and the `varargs.h` facility for writing functions with variable argument lists. The Appendix describes these two facilities, as well as the `stdarg.h` facility (the ANSI C version of `varargs.h`) in detail.

Perhaps the best piece of advice about using library functions is to *use system header files wherever possible*. When the author of a library has provided a header file that accurately describes the functions in that library, it is just plain silly not to use it. This is especially important in ANSI C, where these headers include declarations of argument types as well as result types. In fact, there are some cases in ANSI C where use of system header files is required in order to be assured of getting the right result.

The rest of this chapter explores some problems that programmers seem to have with a few common library functions.

5.1   getchar **returns an integer**

Consider the following program:

```
#include <stdio.h>

main( )
{
        char c;

        while ((c = getchar( )) != EOF)
                putchar(c);
}
```

The getchar function returns the next character from the standard input file, or EOF (a value, defined in stdio.h, which is distinct from any character) if there is no input left. Thus this program looks like it should copy its standard input to its standard output. In fact, it doesn't quite do this.

The reason is that c is declared as a character rather than as an integer. This means that it is impossible for c to hold every possible character as well as EOF.

Thus there are two possibilities. Either some legitimate input character will cause c to take on a value that after truncation is the same as EOF, or it will be impossible for c to have the value EOF at all. In the former case, the program will stop copying in the middle of certain files. In the latter case, the program will go into an infinite loop.

Actually, there is a third case: the program may appear to work by coincidence. Although the result of getchar is truncated to a character value when it is assigned to c, and although the operand of the comparison is supposed to be the truncated value of c and not the result of getchar, surprisingly many compilers do not implement this expression correctly. They properly assign the low-order bits of the value of getchar to c. However, instead of then comparing c to EOF, they compare the entire value of getchar! A compiler that does this will make the sample program shown above appear to work "correctly."

5.2   Updating a sequential file

The standard I/O library on many systems allows a single file to be open simultaneously for input and output:

```
FILE *fp;
fp = fopen(file, "r+");
```

This example opens the file whose name is indicated by the variable file with the intent of both reading and writing it.

Once this has been done, one would think it should be possible to intermix read and write operations freely. Unfortunately, because of efforts to maintain compatibility with programs written before this option became available, this is not so: an input operation may never directly follow an output operation or vice versa without an intervening call to fseek.

The following program fragment appears to update selected records in a sequential file:

```
FILE *fp;
struct record rec;
    . . .
while (fread((char *) &rec, sizeof(rec), 1, fp) == 1) {
        do something to rec
        if (rec must be rewritten) {
                fseek(fp, -(long)sizeof(rec), 1);
                fwrite((char *)&rec, sizeof(rec), 1, fp);
        }
}
```

It looks reasonable enough at first glance: &rec is carefully cast to char * to pass to fread and fwrite, sizeof(rec) is cast to long (fseek demands a long second argument because an int may not be large enough to contain the size of a file; sizeof returns an unsigned value so it is impossible to negate it without first casting it to a signed type). But it still fails, and may fail very subtly indeed.

The problem is that if a record is rewritten — that is, if the fwrite call is executed — the next thing done to the file is the fread at the beginning of the loop. This doesn't work because there is no intervening fseek. The solution is to rewrite it this way:

```
while (fread((char *) &rec, sizeof(rec), 1, fp) == 1) {
        do something to rec
        if (rec must be rewritten) {
                fseek(fp, -(long)sizeof (rec), 1);
                fwrite((char *)&rec, sizeof(rec), 1, fp);
                fseek(fp, 0L, 1);
        }
}
```

The second fseek appears to do nothing, but it puts the file into a state where it can now be read successfully.

5.3   Buffered output and memory allocation

When a program produces output, how important is it that a human be able to see that output immediately? It depends on the program.

For example, if the output is going to a terminal and is asking the person sitting at that terminal to answer a question, it is crucial that the person see the output in order to be able to know what to type. On the other hand, if the output is going to a file, and thence to a line printer, it is only important that all the output get there eventually.

It is often more expensive to arrange for output to appear immediately than it is to save it up for a while and write it later on in a large chunk. For this reason, C implementations typically afford programmers some control over how much output is to be produced before it is actually written.

That control is usually vested in a library function called `setbuf`. If `buf` is a character array of appropriate size, then

```
setbuf(stdout, buf);
```

tells the I/O library that all output written to `stdout` should henceforth use `buf` as an output buffer, and that output directed to `stdout` should not actually be written until `buf` becomes full or until the programmer directs it to be written by calling `fflush`. The appropriate size for such a buffer is defined as `BUFSIZ` in `<stdio.h>`.

Thus, the following program illustrates the obvious way to use `setbuf` in a program that copies its standard input to its standard output:

```
#include <stdio.h>

main()
{
        int c;

        char buf[BUFSIZ];
        setbuf(stdout, buf);

        while ((c = getchar()) != EOF)
                putchar(c);
}
```

Unfortunately, this program is wrong, for a subtle reason. The call to `setbuf` asks the I/O library to use the buffer `buf` to hold characters on their way to the standard output. To see where the trouble lies, ask when `buf` is flushed for the last time. Answer: after the main program has finished, as part of the cleaning up that the library does before handing control back to the operating system. But by that time, `buf` has already been freed!

There are two ways to prevent this sort of trouble. First, make the buffer static, either by declaring it explicitly as static:

```
static char buf[BUFSIZ];
```

or by moving the declaration outside the main program entirely. Another possibility is to allocate the buffer dynamically and never free it:

```
char *malloc();
setbuf(stdout, malloc(BUFSIZ));
```

If you like sleazy programming techniques, notice that there is no need here to check if `malloc` succeeded. If `malloc` fails, it will return a null pointer. This is an acceptable second argument to `setbuf`; it requests that `stdout` be unbuffered. This will work slowly, but it will work.

5.4 Using `errno` for error detection

Many library routines, especially those that deal with the operating system, return a failure indication in an external variable named `errno` when they fail. The obvious way to take advantage of this is wrong:

```
call library function
if (errno)
        complain
```

The trouble is that a library routine that sets `errno` on error is under no obligation to clear it in the absence of an error. Thus it would appear that the following technique would work. It is still wrong:

```
errno = 0;
call library function
if (errno)
        complain
```

Although library routines are not obliged to clear `errno` in the absence of an error, they are not forbidden to set it either. To see why this makes sense, imagine what might happen inside `fopen`. When asked to open a file for output, `fopen` obliterates the file if it is already there and then opens it. This might involve calling some other library function to test for the presence of the file.

Suppose that library function sets `errno` if the file isn't there. Then every time `fopen` opens a file that does not already exist, it has the side effect of setting `errno` even though no error has occurred.

Thus when calling a library function, it is essential to test the value it returns for an error indication *before* examining `errno` to find the cause of the error:

```
call library routine
if  (error return )
        examine errno
```

5.5 The `signal` function

Virtually every C implementation includes the `signal` function as a way of trapping asynchronous events. To use it, write

```
#include <signal.h>
```

to bring in the relevant declarations. To handle a particular signal, write

```
signal(signal type , handler function) ;
```

where *signal type* represents some constant defined in `signal.h` that identifies the kind of signal to be caught and the *handler function* is a function that is to be called whenever the given event occurs.

Signals are truly asynchronous in many implementations. A signal can occur at literally any point during the execution of a C program. In particular, it can occur in the middle of some complicated library function like `malloc`. Thus it is not safe for a signal handler function to call any such library function.

For instance, suppose `malloc` is interrupted by a signal. It is likely that the data structures `malloc` uses to keep track of available memory are only partially updated. If the signal function calls `malloc` again, the result may be to corrupt `malloc`'s data structures completely, with consequent mayhem.

For similar reasons, it is generally unsafe to exit from a signal handler by using `longjmp`: the signal may have occurred while `malloc` or some other library routine had started updating some data structure but not finished it. Thus it appears that the only safe thing for a signal handler to do is to set a flag and return, with the assumption that the main program will test that flag later and discover that a signal has occurred.

But that is not always safe either. When an arithmetic error, such as overflow or division by zero, causes a signal, some machines will re-execute the failing operation after the signal handler returns. There is no portable way to change the operands that the operation will have if it is retried. The likely result in that case is therefore to raise the same signal again immediately. Thus the only portable, reasonably safe thing a signal handler for an arithmetic error can do is to print a message and exit (by using either `longjmp` or `exit`).

The conclusion to draw from this is that signals can be tricky and intrinsically have nonportable aspects. The best defense against problems is to keep signal handlers as simple as possible and group them all together.

That way it will be easy to change them to suit a new system if needed.

Exercise 5-1. When a program terminates abnormally, the last few lines of its output are often lost. Why? What can be done about it? □

Exercise 5-2. The following program copies its input to its output:

```
#include <stdio.h>

main( )
{
        register int c;

        while ((c = getchar( )) != EOF)
                putchar(c);
}
```

Removing the #include statement from this program causes it to fail to compile because EOF is undefined. It is poor practice to do this, but suppose we define EOF by hand:

```
#define EOF -1

main( )
{
        register int c;

        while ((c = getchar( )) != EOF)
                putchar(c);
}
```

This program still works on many systems, but on some it runs much more slowly. Why? □

CHAPTER 6: **THE PREPROCESSOR**

The programs we run are not the programs we write: the C preprocessor transforms them first. The preprocessor gives us ways to abbreviate things that are important for two major reasons (and several minor ones).

First, we may want to be able to change all instances of a particular quantity, such as the size of a table, by changing one number and recompiling the program. The preprocessor makes that easy, even if the number appears in many places in the program: define it once as a *manifest constant* and use it where needed. Moreover, by using the preprocessor it is easy to collect the definitions of these constants together to make them easy to find.

Second, most C implementations impose a significant overhead for each function call. Thus we may want to define things that look like functions but do not have the function call overhead. For example, getchar and putchar are usually implemented as macros to avoid having to call a function for each character of input or output.

Useful as macros are, they can easily confuse programmers who do not realize that *macros act on the text of the program*. That is, macros provide a way of transforming the characters that make up C programs; they do not act on the objects in those programs. Thus it is possible for macros to make something that looks completely ungrammatical into a valid C program, or to transform things that look innocent into monsters.

6.1 Spaces matter in macro definitions

A function without arguments is called by putting parentheses after its name. A macro without arguments is used merely by mentioning its name; parentheses are irrelevant. Once a macro has been defined, this causes no trouble: the preprocessor knows from the macro definition whether to expect arguments after a call.

Defining macros is a little trickier than calling them. For instance, does the definition of f in

```
#define f (x) ((x)-1)
```

take an argument or not? One can imagine answering either way: perhaps f(x) represents

```
((x)-1)
```

or perhaps f represents

```
(x) ((x)-1)
```

In this case, the latter answer is correct because there is a space between f and the (that follows it! Thus, to define f(x) as ((x)-1) one must write

```
#define f(x) ((x)-1)
```

This rule does not apply to macro *calls*, just to macro *definitions*. Thus after the last definition above, f(3) and f (3) both evaluate to 2.

6.2   Macros are not functions

Because macros can be made to appear almost as if they were functions, programmers are sometimes tempted to regard them as truly equivalent. Thus, one sees things like this:

```
#define abs(x) (((x)>=0)?(x):-(x))
```

or:

```
#define max(a,b) ((a)>(b)?(a):(b))
```

Notice all the parentheses in the bodies of these macros. They defend against precedence problems. For instance, suppose abs had been defined this way:

```
#define abs(x) x>0?x:-x
```

and imagine the result of evaluating abs(a-b). The expression

```
abs(a-b)
```

would expand into

```
a-b>0?a-b:-a-b
```

which would give the wrong answer: the subexpression -a-b is equivalent to (-a)-b and not -(a-b) as had been intended. For this reason, it is a good idea in a macro definition to enclose each parameter in parentheses. It is also important to parenthesize the entire result expression to defend against using the macro in a larger expression. Otherwise

```
abs(a)+1
```

would expand into

```
a>0?a:-a+1
```

which is clearly wrong. Defining abs correctly:

```
#define abs(x) ((x)>0?(x):-(x))
```

will cause

```
abs(a-b)
```

to expand correctly into

```
((a-b)>0?(a-b):-(a-b))
```

and will cause

```
abs(a)+1
```

to expand correctly into

```
((a)>0?(a):-(a))+1
```

Even if macro definitions are fully parenthesized, though, an operand that is used twice may be evaluated twice. Thus in the expression max(a,b), if a is greater than b, a will be evaluated twice: once during the comparison, and again to calculate the value max yields.

Not only can this be inefficient, it can also be wrong:

```
biggest = x[0];
i = 1;
while (i < n)
        biggest = max(biggest, x[i++]);
```

This would work fine if max were a true function, but fails with max a macro. To see this, let's initialize some elements of x:

```
x[0] = 2;
x[1] = 3;
x[2] = 1;
```

Look at what happens during the first iteration of the loop. The assignment statement expands into:

```
biggest = ((biggest)>(x[i++])?(biggest):(x[i++]));
```

First, biggest is compared to x[i++]. Since i is 1 and x[1] is 3, the relation is false. As a side effect, i becomes 2.

Because the relation is false, the value of x[i++] is now assigned to biggest. However, i is now 2, so the value assigned to biggest is the value of x[2], which is 1; i is now 3.

One way around these worries is to ensure that the arguments to the max macro have no side effects:

```
biggest = x[0];
for (i = 1; i < n; i++)
        biggest = max(biggest, x[i]);
```

Another is to make max a function, or to do the computation by hand:

```
biggest = x[0];
for (i = 1; i < n; i++)
        if (x[i] > biggest)
                biggest = x[i];
```

Here is another example of the hazards of mixing macros and side effects. Here is a typical definition of the putc macro:

```
#define putc(x,p) \
        (--(p)->_cnt>=0?(*(p)->_ptr++=(x)):_flsbuf(x,p))
```

The first argument to putc is a character to be written to a file; the second argument is a pointer to an internal data structure that describes the file. Notice that the first argument x, which could easily be bound to something like *z++, is carefully evaluated only once, even though it appears in two separate places in the macro body: those two occurrences are on opposite sides of a : operator.

In contrast, the second argument p, which represents the file on which to write, is always evaluated twice. Since it is unusual for the file argument to putc to have side effects, this rarely causes trouble. Nevertheless, the ANSI standard warns that putc may evaluate its second argument twice. Some C implementations are less careful: it is possible to implement a putc that may evaluate its *first* argument more than once. If you give putc an argument with side effects, beware of careless implementations.

As another example, consider the toupper function that appears in many C libraries. It translates a lower-case letter to the corresponding upper-case letter while leaving other characters unchanged. If we assume that all the lower-case letters and all the upper-case letters are contiguous in the machine's collating sequence (with a possible gap between the cases), we get the following function:

```
toupper(int c)
{
        if (c >= 'a' && c <= 'z')
                c += 'A' - 'a';
        return c;
}
```

In most C implementations, the subroutine call overhead is much longer than the actual calculations, so the implementer is tempted to make it a macro:

```
#define toupper(c) \
        ((c)>='a' && (c)<='z'? (c)+('A'-'a'): (c))
```

This is indeed faster than the function in many cases. However, it will surprise anyone who tries to use toupper(*p++).

Another hazard of using macros is that they may generate very large expressions indeed, consuming more space than their user had intended. For example, look again at our definition of max:

```
#define max(a,b) ((a)>(b)?(a):(b))
```

Suppose we want to use this definition to find the largest of a, b, c, and d. If we write the obvious:

```
max(a,max(b,max(c,d)))
```

this expands to:

```
((a)>(((b)>(((c)>(d)?(c):(d)))?(b):(((c)>(d)?(c):(d)))))?
(a):(((b)>(((c)>(d)?(c):(d)))?(b):(((c)>(d)?(c):(d))))))
```

which is surprisingly large. We can make it a little less large by balancing the operands:

```
max(max(a,b),max(c,d))
```

which gives:

```
(((((a)>(b)?(a):(b)))>(((c)>(d)?(c):(d)))?
(((a)>(b)?(a):(b))):(((c)>(d)?(c):(d)))))
```

Somehow, though, it seems easier to write:

```
biggest = a;
if (biggest < b) biggest = b;
if (biggest < c) biggest = c;
if (biggest < d) biggest = d;
```

6.3   Macros are not statements

It is tempting, but surprisingly difficult, to define macros that act like statements. For example, consider the `assert` macro. Its argument is an expression; if that expression is zero it terminates program execution with an appropriate error message. Making it a macro makes it possible for the error message to contain the file name and line number of the failing assertion. In other words,

```
assert(x>y);
```

should do nothing at all if x is greater than y; otherwise it should stop the program.

Here is a first try at it:

```
#define assert(e) if (!e) assert_error(__FILE__,__LINE__)
```

Whoever uses `assert` is expected to supply a semicolon, so no semicolon appears in the definition. The `__FILE__` and `__LINE__` macros are built into the C preprocessor; they expand into the file name and line number on which they were used.

This definition fails subtly in a straightforward context:

```
if (x > 0 && y > 0)
        assert (x > y);
else
        assert (y > x);
```

This is a logical thing to write, but it expands into something like this:

```
if (x > 0 && y > 0)
        if (!(x > y)) assert_error("foo.c", 37);
else
        if (!(y > x)) assert_error("foo.c", 39);
```

Indenting it to show its actual (as opposed to intended) structure gives this:

```
if (x > 0 && y > 0)
        if (!(x > y))
                assert_error("foo.c", 37);
        else
                if (!(y > x))
                        assert_error("foo.c", 39);
```

It is possible to avoid this problem by enclosing the body of the `assert` macro in braces:

```
#define assert(e) \
        { if (!e) assert_error(__FILE__, __LINE__); }
```

This raises a new problem. Our example now expands into:

```
if (x > 0 && y > 0)
        { if (!(x > y)) assert_error("foo.c", 37); };
else
        { if (!(y > x)) assert_error("foo.c", 39); };
```

and the semicolon before the else is a syntax error. One solution to this is to insist that a call to assert not be followed by a semicolon, but using this looks strange:

```
y = distance(p, q);
assert(y > 0)
x = sqrt(y);
```

The right way to define assert is far from obvious: make the body of assert look like an expression and not a statement:

```
#define assert(e) \
        ((void)((e)||_assert_error(__FILE__, __LINE__)))
```

This definition relies on the sequential nature of the || operator. If e is true, the value of

```
(void)((e)||_assert_error(__FILE__, __LINE__))
```

can be determined to be true without evaluating

```
_assert_error(__FILE__, __LINE__)
```

If e is false,

```
_assert_error(__FILE__, __LINE__)
```

must be evaluated; calling assert_error will print an appropriate "assertion failed" message.

6.4   Macros are not type definitions

One common use of macros is to allow the type of several different variables to be stated in one place:

```
#define FOOTYPE struct foo
FOOTYPE a;
FOOTYPE b, c;
```

This lets the programmer change the types of a, b, and c just by changing one line of the program, even if a, b, and c are declared in widely different places.

Using a macro definition for this has the advantage of portability —
any C compiler supports it. But it is better to use a type definition:

```
typedef struct foo FOOTYPE;
```

This defines FOOTYPE as a new type that is equivalent to struct foo.

These two ways of naming a type may appear to be equivalent, but the
typedef is more general. Consider, for example, the following:

```
#define T1 struct foo *
typedef struct foo *T2;
```

These definitions make T1 and T2 conceptually equivalent to a pointer to
a struct foo. But look what happens when we try to use them with
more than one variable:

```
T1 a, b;
T2 c, d;
```

The first declaration gets expanded to

```
struct foo * a, b;
```

This defines a to be a pointer to a structure, but defines b to be a structure (not a pointer). The second declaration, in contrast, defines both c
and d as pointers to structures, because T2 behaves as a true type.

Exercise 6-1. Write a macro version of max with integer arguments that
evaluates its arguments only once. □

Exercise 6-2. Can the "expression"

```
(x) ((x)-1)
```

mentioned in Section 6.1 (page 78) ever be a valid C expression? □

CHAPTER 7

PORTABILITY PITFALLS

C has been implemented by many people to run on many machines. Indeed, one of the reasons to write programs in C in the first place is that it is easy to move them from one programming environment to another.

However, because there are many implementers, they do not all implement precisely the same thing: even the first two C compilers ever written differed significantly from each other. Moreover, different systems have different requirements, so it is reasonable to expect C implementations to differ slightly between one machine and another. The advent of the ANSI standard helps, but is no panacea.

Because the early C implementations shared a common ancestry, that ancestry shaped much of the C library in those implementations. As people started implementing C under various operating systems, they tried to make the library behave in ways that would be familiar to programmers used to the early implementations.

They did not always succeed. What is more, as more people in different parts of the world started working on different C implementations, the exact nature of some of the library functions predictably diverged. Today, a C programmer who wishes to write programs useful in someone else's environment must know about many of these subtle differences.

Portability is therefore a huge subject. In its general form, it far exceeds the scope of this book. Mark Horton treats it in detail in his book, *How to Write Portable Software in C* (Prentice-Hall, to appear). This chapter will address only a few of the most common sources of error, with emphasis on language attributes rather than library attributes.

7.1 Coping with change

As I write this, the ANSI committee is putting the finishing touches on the new C standard. This standard contains many linguistic ideas not yet universal in C compilers. Moreover, even though it is reasonable to expect the vendors of C compilers to move to the new standard, it is not obvious that all C users will quickly upgrade their compilers. New compilers cost money and take time to install. Why replace a compiler that works?

Such change places the author of a C program in a dilemma: should the program use the new features or not? Using them may make the program easier to write and less error-prone, but at the cost of making the program useless on older implementations.

Section 4.4 (page 57) discussed one example of this: the notion of function prototypes. Recall the square function from that section:

```
double
square(double x)
{
        return x * x;
}
```

As written, this function will not compile on many C compilers. Rewriting it in the older style makes it more portable, because the ANSI standard allows the older form as well:

```
double
square(x)
        double x;
{
        return x * x;
}
```

This portability carries a cost. Being consistent about the old usage requires that it be declared as follows in a program that calls it:

```
double square();
```

Leaving out the argument type like this is legal in ANSI C too. Recall that such a declaration says nothing at all about the argument types. That means that a call with the wrong argument type will fail quietly:

```
double square();

main()
{
        printf("%g\n"; square(3));
}
```

Because the declaration of square says nothing about argument types, it is impossible when compiling main to know that the argument to square should be double and not int. Thus this program will print garbage. The way to detect problems of this sort is to use the lint program mentioned in Section 4.0 (page 53) if it is available.

If the program had been written this way:

```
double square(double);

main()
{
        printf("%g\n", square(3));
}
```

then 3 would have been converted automatically from int to double. Alternatively, the program could have passed a double argument explicitly:

```
double square();

main()
{
        printf("%g\n", square(3.0));
}
```

and it would still work. This latter style will work even in older compilers that do not allow function declarations to include argument types.

Many portability decisions have this flavor. Should a programmer use some new or specialized facility or not? Using it may bring great convenience, but only at the cost of cutting off part of the potential audience for the program.

There are no easy answers to these questions. Programs tend to last longer than their authors ever dreamed, even when written only for the authors' own use. Thus it is not enough to do what works now and ignore the future. Yet we have just seen that trying to be as portable as possible can be expensive by denying us today's benefits in order to live with yesterday's tools. The best we can do about decisions like these is to admit that they *are* decisions and not let them be made by accident.

7.2   What's in a name?

Some C implementations treat all the characters of an identifier as being significant. Others quietly chop the tails off long identifiers. Linkers may impose their own restrictions on the kinds of names they can handle, such as allowing only upper-case letters in external names. When faced with such a restriction, it is reasonable for a C implementer to force all external names to upper case. In fact, all ANSI C guarantees is that the implementation will distinguish external names that differ in the first six characters. For the purpose of this definition, upper-case letters do not differ from the corresponding lower-case letters.

Because of this, it is important to be careful when choosing external identifiers in programs intended to be portable. Having two functions named, say, `print_fields` and `print_float` would not be a very good idea, nor would it be wise to have `State` and `STATE`.

As a striking example, consider the following function:

```
char *
Malloc(unsigned n)
{
        char *p, *malloc(unsigned);
        p = malloc(n);
        if (p == NULL)
                panic("out of memory");
        return p;
}
```

This is a simple way of ensuring that running out of memory will not go undetected. The idea is for a program to allocate memory by calling `Malloc` instead of `malloc`. If `malloc` ever fails, the result will be to call `panic` which will presumably terminate the program with an appropriate error message. This makes it unnecessary for the client program to check every call to `malloc` itself.

Consider, however, what happens when this function is used with a C implementation that ignores case distinctions in external identifiers. In effect, the names `malloc` and `Malloc` become equivalent. In other words, the library function `malloc` is effectively replaced by the `Malloc` function above, which when it calls `malloc` is really calling itself. The result, of course, is that the first attempt to allocate memory results in a recursion loop and consequent mayhem, even though the function will work on an implementation that preserves case distinctions.

7.3   How big is an integer?

C provides the programmer with three sizes of integers: short, plain, and long, and with characters, which behave as if they were small integers. The language definition guarantees a few things about the relative sizes of the various kinds of integer:

1. The three sizes of integers are nondecreasing. That is, a short integer can contain only values that will also fit in a plain integer and a plain integer can contain only values that will also fit in a long integer. An implementation need not actually support three different sizes of integers, but it may not make short integers larger than plain integers or plain integers larger than long integers.

2. An ordinary integer is large enough to contain any array subscript.

3. The size of a character is natural for the particular hardware.

Most modern machines have 8-bit characters, though a few have 9-bit characters. However, there is a growing number of implementations with 16-bit characters, to be able to handle the large character sets of languages like Japanese.

The ANSI standard requires long integers to be at least 32 bits and short or ordinary integers to be at least 16 bits. Because most machines have 8-bit characters, and the most convenient integer sizes for such machines are 16 and 32 bits, virtually all older C compilers observe these limits as well.

What does this all mean in practice? The most important thing is that one cannot count on having any particular precision available. Informally, one can probably expect 16 bits for a short or an ordinary integer, and 32 bits for a long integer, but not even those sizes are guaranteed. One can certainly use ordinary integers to express table sizes and subscripts, but what about a variable that must be able to hold values up to ten million?

The most portable way to define such a variable is probably to declare it as long, but in such circumstances it is often clearer to define a "new" type:

```
typedef long tenmil;
```

Moreover, one can use this type to declare all variables of that width and know that, at worst, one will have to change a single type definition to get all those variables to be the right type.

7.4   Are characters signed or unsigned?

Most modern computers support 8-bit characters, so most modern C compilers implement characters as 8-bit integers. However, not all compilers interpret those 8-bit quantities the same way.

The issue becomes important only when converting a char quantity to a larger integer. Going the other way, the results are well-defined: excess bits are simply discarded. But a compiler converting a char to an int has a choice: should it treat the char as a signed or an unsigned quantity? If the former, it should expand the char to an int by replicating the sign bit; if the latter, it should fill the extra bit positions with zeroes.

The results of this decision are important to virtually anyone who deals with characters with their high-order bits turned on. It determines whether 8-bit characters are going to be considered to range from −128 through 127 or from 0 through 255. This, in turn, affects the way a programmer will design things like hash tables and translate tables.

If you care whether a character value with the high-order bit on is treated as a negative number, you should probably declare it as unsigned char. Such values are guaranteed to be zero-extended when converted to integer, whereas ordinary char variables may be signed in one implementation and unsigned in another.

Incidentally, it is a common misconception that if c is a character variable, one can obtain the unsigned integer equivalent of c by writing (unsigned) c. This fails because when converting a char quantity to unsigned, it is converted to int first, with possibly unexpected results.

The right way to do it is (unsigned char) c. Converting an unsigned char to an integer type will give an unsigned int without going through int first.

7.5 Shift operators

Two questions seem to cause trouble for people who use shift operators:

1. In a right shift, are vacated bits filled with zeroes or copies of the sign bit?

2. What values are permitted for the shift count?

The answer to the first question is simple but sometimes implementation-dependent. If the item being shifted is unsigned, zeroes are shifted in. If the item is signed, the implementation is permitted to fill vacated bit positions either with zeroes or with copies of the sign bit. If you care about vacated bits in a right shift, declare the variable in question as unsigned. You are then entitled to assume that vacated bits will be set to zero.

The answer to the second question is also simple: if the item being shifted is n bits long, then the shift count must be greater than or equal to zero and *strictly* less than n. Thus, it is not possible to shift all the bits out of a value in a single operation. The purpose of this restriction is to allow efficient implementation on hardware with the corresponding restriction.

For example, if an int is 32 bits, and n is an int, it is legal to write n<<31 and n<<0 but not n<<32 or n<<-1.

Note that a right shift of a signed integer is generally not equivalent to division by a power of two, even if the implementation copies the sign into vacated bits. To prove this, consider that the value of (-1)>>1 cannot possibly be zero, but (-1)/2 is zero in most implementations. This suggests that writing a division instead of a shift may result in a surprisingly slow program. For instance, it is equivalent, and much faster, to execute

```
    mid = (low + high) >> 1;
```

instead of

```
    mid = (low + high) / 2;
```

if low+high is known to be nonnegative.

7.6 Memory location zero

A null pointer does not point to any object. Thus it is illegal to use a null pointer for any purposes other than assignment and comparison. For example, the value of strcmp(p,q) is undefined if p or q is a null pointer.

What actually happens in this case varies from one C implementation to another. Some implementations impose hardware read protection on location 0. A program that misuses a null pointer on such an implementation will fail immediately. Other implementations allow location 0 to be read but not written. In this case, a null pointer will appear to point to some character string, usually garbage. Other implementations allow location 0 to be written as well as read. Misusing a null pointer on such an implementation may well overwrite part of the operating system, causing complete mayhem.

Strictly speaking, this is not a portability problem: the effect of misusing a null pointer is undefined in all C programs. However, such programs can easily appear to work on one implementation, with the trouble not showing up until the program is moved to another machine.

The easiest way to detect these problems is to run your programs on a machine that prohibits reading location 0. The following program will discover how an implementation treats location 0:

```
    #include <stdio.h>

    main()
    {
            char *p;

            p = NULL;
            printf("Location 0 contains %d\n", *p);
    }
```

This program will fail on a machine that prohibits reading location 0. Otherwise it will say, in decimal form, what character appears to occupy location 0.

7.7 How does division truncate?

Suppose we divide a by b to give a quotient q and remainder r:

```
q = a / b;
r = a % b;
```

For the moment, suppose also that b>0.

What relationships might we want to hold between a, b, p, and q?

1. Most important, we want q*b + r == a, because this is the relation that defines the remainder.

2. If we change the sign of a, we want that to change the sign of q, but not the magnitude.

3. When b>0, we want to ensure that r>=0 and r<b. For instance, if the remainder is being used as an index to a hash table, it is important to be able to know that it will always be a valid index.

These three properties are clearly desirable for integer division and remainder operations. Unfortunately, *they cannot all be true at once*.

Consider 3/2, giving a quotient of 1 and a remainder of 1. This satisfies property 1. What should be the value of (-3)/2? Property 2 suggests that it should be -1, but if that is so, the remainder must *also* be -1, which violates property 3. Alternatively, we can satisfy property 3 by making the remainder 1, in which case property 1 demands that the quotient be -2. This violates property 2.

Thus C, and any language that implements truncating integer division, must give up at least one of these three principles. Most programming languages give up number 3, saying instead that the remainder has the same sign as the dividend. This makes it possible to preserve properties 1 and 2. Most C implementations do this in practice, also.

However, the C language definition guarantees only property 1, along with the property that $|r|<|b|$ and that $r \geqslant 0$ whenever $a \geqslant 0$ and $b > 0$. This property is less restrictive than either property 2 or property 3.

Despite its sometimes unwanted flexibility, the C definition is enough that we can make integer division do what we want provided that we know what we want. Suppose, for example, that we have a number n that represents some function of the characters in an identifier, and we want to use division to obtain a hash table entry h such that $0 \leqslant h < HASHSIZE$. If we know that n is never negative, we simply write

```
h = n % HASHSIZE;
```

However, if n might be negative, this is not good enough, because h might also be negative. However, we know that $h > -HASHSIZE$, so we can write:

```
h = n % HASHSIZE;
if (h < 0)
        h += HASHSIZE;
```

Better yet, design the program to avoid negative values of n in the first place and declare n as unsigned.

7.8   How big is a random number?

When the only C implementation ran on the PDP-11 computer, there was a function called rand that returned a (pseudo-) random nonnegative integer. PDP-11 integers were 16 bits long, including the sign, so rand would return an integer between 0 and $2^{15}-1$.

When C was implemented on the VAX-11, integers were 32 bits long. This raised an implementation question: what should be the range of the rand function on the VAX-11?

This question was answered differently in two parallel implementation efforts. When the people at the University of California at Berkeley did their C implementation, they took the view that rand should return a value that ranges over all possible nonnegative integers, so their version of rand returns an integer between 0 and $2^{31}-1$.

The people at AT&T, on the other hand, decided that a PDP-11 program that expected the result of rand to be less than 2^{15} would be easier to transport to a VAX-11 if the rand function returned a value between 0 and 2^{15} there, too.

As a result, it is now difficult to write a program that uses rand without tailoring it to the implementation. ANSI C defines a constant RAND_MAX equal to the largest random number, but earlier C implementations generally do not have it.

7.9   Case conversion

The toupper and tolower functions have a similar history. They were originally written as macros:

```
#define toupper(c) ((c)+'A'-'a')
#define tolower(c) ((c)+'a'-'A')
```

When given a lower-case letter as input toupper yields the corresponding upper-case letter. The tolower function does the opposite. Both these macros depend on the implementation's character set to the extent that they demand that the difference between an upper-case letter and the corresponding lower-case letter be the same constant for all letters. This assumption is valid for both the ASCII and EBCDIC character sets, and probably isn't too dangerous, because the nonportability of these macro definitions can be encapsulated in the single file that contains them.

These macros do have one disadvantage, though: when given something that is not a letter of the appropriate case, they return garbage. Thus, the following innocent program fragment to convert a file to lower case doesn't work with these macros:

```
int c;
while ((c = getchar()) != EOF)
        putchar(tolower(c));
```

Instead, one must write:

```
int c;
while ((c = getchar()) != EOF)
        putchar(isupper(c)? tolower(c): c);
```

At one point, an enterprising soul in AT&T software development noticed that most uses of toupper and tolower were preceded by tests to ensure that their arguments were appropriate. He considered rewriting the macros this way:

```
#define toupper(c) ((c)>='a'&&(c)<='z'?(c)+'A'-'a':(c))
#define tolower(c) ((c)>='A'&&(c)<='Z'?(c)+'a'-'A':(c))
```

but realized that this would cause c to be evaluated anywhere between one and three times for each call, which would play havoc with expressions like toupper(*p++). Instead, he decided to rewrite toupper and tolower as functions. The toupper function now looked something like this:

```
int
toupper(int c)
{
        if (c >= 'a' && c <= 'z')
                return c + 'A' - 'a';
        return c;
}
```

and tolower looked similar.

This change had the advantage of robustness, at the cost of introducing function call overhead into each use of these functions. Our hero realized that some people might not be willing to pay the cost of this overhead, so he re-introduced the macros with new names:

```
#define _toupper(c) ((c)+'A'-'a')
#define _tolower(c) ((c)+'a'-'A')
```

This gave users a choice of convenience or speed.

There was just one problem in all this: the people at Berkeley never followed suit, nor did some other C implementers. This means that a program written on an AT&T system that uses toupper or tolower, and assumes that it will be able to pass an argument that is not a letter of the appropriate case, may stop working on some other C implementation. This sort of failure is very hard to trace for someone who does not know this bit of history.

7.10   Free first, then reallocate?

Most C implementations provide users with three memory allocation functions called malloc, realloc, and free. Calling malloc(n) returns a pointer to n characters of newly-allocated memory that the programmer can use. Giving free a pointer to memory previously returned by malloc makes that memory available for reuse. Calling realloc with a pointer to an allocated area and a new size stretches or shrinks the memory to the new size, possibly copying it in the process.

Things were not always this way. The seventh edition of the reference manual for the UNIX system described slightly different behavior:

> *Realloc* changes the size of the block pointed to by *ptr* to *size* bytes and returns a pointer to the (possibly moved) block. The contents will be unchanged up to the lesser of the new and old sizes.

> *Realloc* also works if *ptr* points to a block freed since the last call of *malloc, realloc,* or *calloc;* thus sequences of *free, malloc,* and *realloc* can exploit the search strategy of *malloc* to do storage compaction.

In other words, this implementation allowed a memory area to be reallocated *after it had been freed,* as long as that reallocation was done quickly enough. Thus, the following is legal under the Seventh Edition system:

```
free(p);
p = realloc(p, newsize);
```

On a system with this idiosyncrasy, one can free all the elements of a list by the following curious method:

```
for (p = head; p != NULL; p = p->next)
    free((char *) p);
```

without worrying that the call to *free* might invalidate p->next.

Needless to say, this technique is not recommended, if only because not all C implementations preserve memory long enough after it has been freed. However, the Seventh Edition manual leaves one thing unstated: an earlier implementation of realloc actually *required* that the

area given to it for reallocation be freed first. For this reason, there are
still some C programs floating around that free memory first and then
reallocate it. This is something to watch out for when moving a very old
C program to a new implementation.

7.11   An example of portability problems

Let's look at a problem that has been solved many times by many people.
The following program takes two arguments: a long integer and a
(pointer to a) function. It converts the integer to decimal and calls the
function with each character of the decimal representation:

```
void
printnum(long n, void (*p)())
{
        if (n < 0) {
                (*p)('-');
                n = -n;
        }
        if (n >= 10)
                printnum(n/10, p);
        (*p) ((int)(n % 10) + '0');
}
```

This program is fairly straightforward. First we check if n is negative;
if so, we print a sign and make n positive. Next, we test if $n \geqslant 10$. If so,
its decimal representation has two or more digits, so we call printnum
recursively to print all but the last digit. Finally, we print the last digit,
casting the expression n%10 to int so that the right type of argument
will be handed to *p.† This is unnecessary in ANSI C but defends
against the possibility of someone translating it for an older implementation by simply rewriting the function header.

This program, for all its simplicity, has several portability problems.
The first is the method it uses to convert the low-order decimal digit of n
to character form. Using n%10 to get the value of the low-order digit is
fine, but adding '0' to it to get the corresponding character representation is not. This addition assumes that the machine collating sequence
has all the digits in sequence with no gaps, so that '0'+5 has the same
value as '5', and so on. This assumption, while true of the ASCII and

---

† The technical report on which this book was based had

```
        (*p) (n % 10 + '0');
```

as the last statement in printnum. This will work only on a machine in which int and
long have the same internal representation.

EBCDIC character sets and of any ANSI-conforming implementation, might not be true for some machines. The way to avoid that problem is to use a table. Because a string constant represents a character array, it is legal to use it in place of an array name. Thus the surprising expression

```
"0123456789"[n % 10]
```

in the example below is legal:

```
void
printnum(long n, void (*p)())
{
        if (n < 0) {
                (*p)('-');
                n = -n;
        }
        if (n >= 10)
                printnum(n/10, p);
        (*p)("0123456789"[n % 10]);
}
```

The next problem involves what happens if $n < 0$. The program prints a negative sign and sets n to -n. This assignment might overflow, because 2's complement machines generally allow more negative values than positive values to be represented. In particular, if a (long) integer is k bits plus one extra bit for the sign, -2^k can be represented but 2^k cannot.

There are several ways around this problem. The most obvious one is to assign -n to an unsigned long value and be done with it. But we cannot evaluate -n because it might overflow!

In both 1's complement and 2's complement machines, changing the sign of a *positive* integer is guaranteed not to overflow. The only trouble comes when changing the sign of a *negative* value. Therefore, we can avoid trouble by making sure we do not attempt to make n positive.

Of course, once we have printed the sign of a negative value, we would like to be able to treat negative and positive numbers the same way. The way to do that is to force n to be negative after printing the sign, and to do all our arithmetic with negative values. If we do this, we will have to ensure that the part of the program that prints the sign is executed only once; the easiest way to do that is to split the program into two functions. The printnum function now just checks if the number being printed is negative; if so it prints a negative sign. In either case, it calls printneg with the negative absolute value of n. The printneg function now caters to the fact n will always be negative or zero:

```
void
printneg(long n, void (*p)())
{
        if (n <= -10)
                printneg(n/10, p);
        (*p)("0123456789"[-(n % 10)]);
}

void
printnum(long n, void (*p)())
{
        if (n < 0) {
                (*p)('-');
                printneg(n, p);
        } else
                printneg(-n, p);

}
```

This still doesn't quite work. We have used n/10 and n%10 to represent the leading digits and the trailing digit of n (with suitable sign changes). Recall that integer division behaves in a somewhat implementation-dependent way when one of the operands is negative. For that reason, it might actually be that n%10 is positive! In that case, -(n%10) would be negative, and we would run off the end of our digit array.

We cater to this problem by creating two temporary variables to hold the quotient and remainder. After we do the division, we check that the remainder is in range and adjust both variables if not. The printnum function has not changed, so we show only printneg:

```
void
printneg(long n, void (*p)())
{
        long q;
        int r;

        q = n / 10;
        r = n % 10;
        if (r > 0) {
                r -= 10;
                q++;
        }
        if (n <= -10)
                printneg(q, p);
        (*p)("0123456789"[-r]);
}
```

This looks like a lot of work to cater to portability.

Why bother? Because we live in a world of constantly changing programming environments. Despite its intangibility, most software will outlast the hardware on which it runs. Moreover, it is not always easy to predict the nature of future hardware. Portable software is lasting software.

Portable software is also more likely to be correct. Much of the effort in this example actually went into ensuring that printnum would work properly even when presented with the most negative possible value as its argument. I've seen several commercial software products that blow up in precisely such a situation.

Exercise 7-1. Section 7.3 (page 89) said that a machine with 8-bit characters would be most likely to have 16-bit or 32-bit integers. Why? □

Exercise 7-2. Write a portable version of the atol function, which takes a pointer to a null-terminated character string as its argument and returns the corresponding long value. Assume:

- The input will always represent a valid long integer, so atol need not check for the input being out of bounds;

- The only valid input characters are digits and + and – signs. The input ends at the first invalid character. □

CHAPTER 8: **ADVICE AND ANSWERS**

You have just finished a tour through some of the ways that C programmers can hurt themselves. Like many of the people who read early drafts of this book, you are probably wondering: "How can I avoid these problems?"

Perhaps the most important avoidance technique is to *know what you're doing*. The most irritating problems stem from programs that appear to work but have hidden problems. Because these problems are hidden, the easiest way to detect them is by careful thought in advance. Fiddling with a program until it appears to work is a reliable way of obtaining a program that almost works.

The most eloquent statement of this I have seen appears, of all places, in the construction manual for a harpsichord. It was written by David Jacques Way, who clearly appreciates the importance of confident knowledge, and with whose kind permission I reprint it:

'Thinking' is the cause of all error; I can prove this by the fact that whoever makes a mistake always says, "Oh, but I thought...." Never mind this kind of thinking — before you glue anything together you must know. Put the parts together without glue (called a 'dry run'), study how they fit, and check with your drawing, which shows how everything fits.

And after you have put something together with glue, check it again. I've heard the sad story so many times: "Last night I did so and so, and this morning when I looked at it...."

Dear builder, if you had looked at it last night you could still have taken it apart and put things right. Many of you are building in your spare time, so the temptation is great to work far into the night. But if I can believe my telephone calls, most mistakes are made the last thing before you go to bed. So go to bed before you do the last thing.

This advice is remarkably relevant to programming if one thinks of "putting it together with glue" as combining several small pieces into a bigger program. Understanding how the pieces are going to fit before actually fitting them is one of the keys to a reliable result.

Such understanding is particularly important under time pressure. Near the end of a long debugging session, it becomes tempting to try things almost at random and stop as soon as something seems to work. That way lies disaster.

8.1 Advice

Here are some more general thoughts about error reduction.

Don't talk yourself into seeing what isn't there. Errors can be seductive. For instance, the example in Section 1.1 (page 6) looked a little different in the technical report that eventually grew into this book:

```
while (c == '\t' ¦¦ c = ' ' ¦¦ c == '\n')
        c = getc(f);
```

As shown, this example is not valid C. The precedence of = is lowest of any operator in the while clause, so it would have to be interpreted this way:

```
while ((c == '\t' ¦¦ c) = (' ' ¦¦ c == '\n'))
        c = getc(f);
```

This, of course, is invalid:

```
(c == '\t' ¦¦ c)
```

cannot stand on the left-hand side of an assignment. Thousands of people saw this example, but no one noticed it until Rob Pike finally pointed it out to me.

When I started writing the book, I left the comments from readers of the technical report until I was nearly done. Thus the erroneous example above made it into the draft that went around for review inside Bell Labs and again in the draft that Addison-Wesley sent out for review. Not one single reviewer noticed the error.

Make your intentions plain. When you write one thing that might be mistaken for another, use parentheses or other methods to make sure your intent is clear. Not only will this help you understand what you mean when you come back to the program, but it will also make things easier if someone else has to look at it later.

It is sometimes possible to say things in a way that anticipates likely mistakes. For example, some programmers put constants on the left of equality comparisons. That is, instead of saying

```
while (c == '\t' || c == ' ' || c == '\n')
        c = getc(f);
```

they say

```
while ('\t' == c || ' ' == c || '\n' == c)
        c = getc(f);
```

This way, writing = instead of == elicits a compiler diagnostic:

```
while ('\t' = c || ' ' == c || '\n' == c)
        c = getc(f);
```

is invalid because it tries to assign a value to '\t'.

Look at trivial cases. This applies both to figuring out how programs work and to testing them. So many programs fail when some part of their input is empty or has only one element that those are the cases to try first.

This applies to program design too. When designing a program, ask yourself what it will do with an empty collection of input data.

Use asymmetric bounds. Read again the discussion in Section 3.6 (page 36) about representing ranges. The fact that C subscripts start from zero makes all kinds of counting problems easier once you understand how to handle them.

Bugs lurk in dark corners. C implementations all differ slightly from each other. Stick to the well-known parts of the language. By doing that, you will make it easier to move your program to a new machine or compiler and make it less likely that you will run into compiler bugs.

Recall, for instance, that the discussion of arrays and pointers in Section 3.1 (page 31) stopped with issues still unexplored. Any program that actually depends on the implementation getting all those details right is likely to stop working at some point.

It may be worth defending against sloppy library implementations, too. I had a lot of trouble moving a program once from one machine to another, because that program thought it could call printf with a format string several thousand characters long. Nothing wrong with that, of course, except that some implementations of printf can't handle it.

This advice is especially important if you are thinking of using some feature supported by only one vendor. Remember, your programs may well outlast your machine.

Program defensively. Don't assume any more about your users or your implementation than you have to. I recall one conversation I had with

someone for whom I was building a system that went something like
this:

"What codes can appear in this part of this record?"

"The possible codes are X, Y, and Z."

"What if something else appears here?"

"That can't happen."

"Well, the program has to do *something* if it happens. What should
it do?"

"I don't care what it does."

"You really don't care?"

"Right."

"Then you won't mind if I have it delete the entire database if it
ever detects a code other than X, Y, or Z here?"

"Don't be absurd. You can't go deleting the whole database!"

"Then you *do* care what it does. So what would you like it to do?"

Things that "can't happen" sometimes happen anyway. A robust program will defend against them.

   It would be nice if C implementations could catch more programming
errors. Unfortunately that is difficult for several reasons. The most
important is probably historical: people have tended to use C for things
that formerly were done in assembly language. Therefore many C programs have parts that deliberately do things that, strictly speaking, are
outside what the language permits. Obvious examples are things like
operating systems. A strictly checking C implementation would have to
have some kind of "escape route" that would permit such programs to do
the machine-specific things they need to do, while still checking strictly
the parts of the programs that are intended to be portable.

   Moreover, some things are intrinsically hard to check. Consider this
function:

```
void
set(int *p, int n)
{
        *p = n;
}
```

Is this valid or not? The answer, of course, is that is it impossible to know out of context. If it is called this way:

```
int a[10];
set(a+5, 37);
```

it is valid, but if it is called this way

```
int a[10];
set(a+10, 37);
```

it isn't. And yet nothing is wrong with the latter fragment by itself: ANSI C allows a program to generate the address of the location just past the end of an array. So a C implementation that catches this sort of error must be clever indeed.

That is not to say that C implementations that check more thoroughly for errors are impossible — they aren't. In fact, there are a few on the market. But no implementation can find all the errors in a program.

8.2 Answers

0–1 Would you buy an automobile made by a company with a high proportion of recalls? Would that change if they told you they had cleaned up their act? What does it *really* cost for your users to find your bugs for you?

Reputation is an important factor in our choice of one product over another. And once a reputation is lost it is hard to regain. It takes a while to decide whether the high quality of the firm's recent products is for real or just a fluke.

Most people would not knowingly buy a product that they expected to have significant design defects — except if it is a software product. Most people write at least some of their programs for use by others. People *expect* software not to work. Surprise them.

0–2 How many fence posts 10 feet apart do you need to support 100 feet of fence?

Eleven. There are 10 segments of fence, but 11 posts. Count them yourself. Section 3.6 (page 36) has more to say about the relevance of this problem to programming errors.

0–3   Have you ever cut yourself with a knife while cooking? How could cooking knives be made safer? Would you want to use a knife that had been modified that way?

It is easier to think of ways to make complicated tools safer than simple ones. Food processors always have interlocks to prevent their users from losing fingers. But knives don't: adding finger protection to such a simple, flexible tool would rob it of its simplicity. In fact, the result might look more like a food processor than a knife.

Making it hard to do stupid things often makes it hard to do smart ones too.

1–1   Some C compilers allow nested comments. Write a C program that determines whether it is being run on such a compiler *without* generating any error messages. In other words, the program should be valid under both comment rules, but should do something different in each. *Hint.* A comment symbol /* inside a quoted string is just part of the string; a double quote "" inside a comment is part of the comment.

In order to tell if comments nest, it is necessary to find some sequence of symbols that is valid under both interpretations but means different things in each. Of necessity, such a sequence involves nested comments; let us begin that way:

    /* /* */

Whatever follows this will be part of a comment in a nesting implementation, but taken for real in a nonnesting implementation. One might therefore imagine appending a close comment symbol in quotes:

    /* /* */ " */ "

If comments nest, this is equivalent to one quote. If not, it is a literal string. We can therefore continue with an open comment and another quote:

    /* /* */ " */ " /* "

If comments nest, this is a quoted open comment symbol. If not, it is a quoted close comment symbol, followed by an unclosed comment. We must simply close that comment:

    /* /* */ " */ " /* " /* */

This expression is equivalent to " */ " if comments nest and " /* " if they don't.

After I solved this problem in essentially the form shown above, Doug

McIlroy found the following astonishing solution:

```
/*/*/0*/**/1
```

This takes advantage of the "maximal munch" rule. If comments nest, it is interpreted this way:

```
/* /* /0 */ * */ 1
```

The two /* symbols match the two */ symbols, so the value of this is 1. If comments do not nest, a /* in a comment is ignored. Thus even a / in a comment has no special meaning; the expression is thus interpreted this way:

```
/* / */ 0 * /* */ 1
```

0*1 evaluates to 0.

1-2 If you were writing a C compiler, would you make it possible for users to nest comments? If you were using a C compiler that permitted nested comments, would you use that facility? Does your answer to the second question affect your answer to the first?

Nested comments are useful for removing a block of code temporarily: begin a comment before the code in question and end it after it. That does have a disadvantage, though: if a large block is removed that way, it is easy to fail to notice that it has been removed.

However, the C language definition says that comments do not nest, so a faithful implementer has no choice. Moreover, a programmer who relies on nested comments will produce programs that will fail to work on many compilers. Thus any use of nested comments would necessarily be limited to programs not intended for distribution in source form. Moreover, such programs would run the risk of failing on new or revised C implementations.

For that reason, I would not implement nested comments if I were writing a C compiler, and I would not use them if my compiler had them. Of course, you must make up your own mind.

1-3 Why does n-->0 mean n-- > 0 and not n- -> 0?

Because of the maximal munch rule, -- is determined to be a single token before the > is seen.

1-4 What does a+++++b mean?

The only meaningful way to parse this is

```
a ++ + ++ b
```

However, the maximal munch rule requires it to be broken down as

```
a ++ ++ + b
```

This is syntactically invalid: it is equivalent to

```
((a++)++) + b
```

but the result of a++ is not an lvalue and hence is not acceptable as an operand of ++. Thus the rules for resolving *lexical* ambiguity make it impossible to resolve this example in a way that is *syntactically* meaningful. In practice, of course, the prudent thing to do is to avoid constructions like this unless you are absolutely certain what they mean.

2–1   C permits an extra comma in an initializer list:

```
int days[] = { 31, 28, 31, 30, 31, 30,
               31, 31, 30, 31, 30, 31, };
```

Why is this useful?

After rewriting the example slightly,

```
int days[] = {
        31, 28, 31, 30, 31, 30,
        31, 31, 30, 31, 30, 31,
};
```

it is now easy to see that each line of the initializer list ends with a comma. Because every line is syntactically similar, it is much easier to use automatic tools like editors to deal with large initialization lists.

2–2   We have seen several problems caused by the fact that C statements end with semicolons. While it is too late to change that now, it is fun to speculate about other ways of separating statements. How do other languages do it? Do those methods have their own pitfalls?

Fortran and Snobol statements both end at the end of the line; both languages allow a statement to span more than one line by so indicating on the *second* and subsequent lines of the statement. In Fortran, the indication is a non-blank character in character position 6 of the line (positions 0–5 are reserved for labels); in Snobol, the indication is a . or + in position 1.

It seems a little strange for the meaning of a line to be affected by the next line. A few languages therefore use some kind of indication on line *n* that line *n*+1 should be considered part of the same statement. The

UNIX system Shell, for example, uses a \ character at the end of the line to indicate that the next line is part of the same statement, and C uses the same convention in the preprocessor and inside character strings. Other languages, such as Awk and Ratfor, say that a statement is continued if it ends with something that demands to be followed, such as an operator or an open parenthesis. Such schemes seem to work well in practice, though they can be hard to define rigorously.

3-1 Suppose it were illegal even to generate the address of an array element that is out of bounds. How would the bufwrite programs in Section 3.6 (page 39) look?

The bufwrite programs assume that it is possible to return with the buffer completely full and flush it the next time bufwrite is called. If bufptr may not point beyond the buffer, this problem suddenly becomes messy: how should we indicate that the buffer is full?

The least inconvenient solution seems to be to avoid leaving the buffer full when bufwrite returns. To do this, we treat the last character to enter the buffer as a special case.

We must also avoid incrementing p until we know that it does not already point to the last element of some array. In effect, we must not increment p after fetching the last input character. We do this here with an extra test each time through the loop; the alternative would be to duplicate the whole loop:

```
void
bufwrite(char *p, int n)
{
        while (--n >= 0) {
                if (bufptr == &buffer[N-1]) {
                        *bufptr = *p;
                        flushbuffer();
                } else
                        *bufptr++ = *p;
                if (n > 0)
                        p++;
        }
}
```

We carefully avoid incrementing bufptr when the buffer is full to avoid generating the illegal address of buffer[N].

The second version of bufwrite becomes even messier. We know at entry that there is at least one character available in the buffer, so we never have to flush at the beginning; but we may have to flush at the end. And again we must avoid incrementing p the last time through the loop:

```
void
bufwrite(char *p, int n)
{
        while (n > 0) {
                int k, rem;
                rem = N - (bufptr - buffer);
                k = n > rem? rem: n;
                memcpy(bufptr, p, k);
                if (k == rem)
                        flushbuffer();
                else
                        bufptr += k;
                n -= k;
                if (n)
                        p += k;
        }
}
```

We compare k, the number of characters we will copy in the current
iteration, with rem, the number of characters remaining free in the
buffer, to see if the buffer will be full after the copy and needs flushing.
We check for the last time through the loop by comparing n to 0 before
incrementing p.

3–2   Compare the last version of flush shown in Section 3.6 (page 45)
       with this one:

```
void
flush()
{
        int row;
        int k = bufptr - buffer;
        if (k > NROWS)
                k = NROWS;
        for (row = 0; row < k; row++) {
                int *p;
                for (p = buffer+row; p < bufptr;
                                p += NROWS)
                        printnum(*p);
                printnl();
        }
        if (k > 0)
                printpage();
}
```

The difference between these two versions is that the one shown here includes only the call to `printpage` in the test for k>0, where the version in Chapter 3 includes the entire `for` loop as well. That version might be translated into English as: "If there is anything to print, print it and then start a new page." The present version instead says, "Print whatever is left, and start a new page if there was anything." The role of k in the `for` loop above is a little less obvious than the version in Chapter 3. There, it was immediately clear that the loop is skipped if k is zero.

Although these two programs are technically equivalent, they express slightly different intentions. The better one is whichever one expresses the programmer's actual intention more closely.

3–3 Write a function to do a binary search in a sorted table of integers. Its input is a pointer to the beginning of the table, a count of the elements in the table, and a value to be sought. Its output is a pointer to the element sought or a NULL pointer if the element is not present.

Binary searches are conceptually very simple, but in practice people often get them wrong. We will develop two versions here, both using asymmetric bounds. The first uses subscripts; the second uses pointers.

Assume that x, the element sought, is element number k of the array if it's there at all. Initially, all we know about k is that $0 \leqslant k < n$. Our aim is to narrow that range until we find the element we seek or determine that it isn't there.

In order to do this, we compare x to the element in the middle of the range. If x is equal to that element, we're done. Otherwise we can reduce the range by eliminating all the elements on the "wrong" side of the one we examined. Here is a picture of the state of affairs during the search:

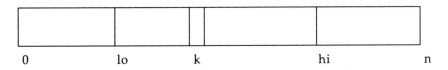

At any given time, we will consider the asymmetric range between lo and hi. That is, we will require that $lo \leqslant k < hi$. If ever $lo = hi$, the range has shrunk to nothing and we know that x is not in the table.

If $lo < hi$, there is at least one element in the range. We will set mid to the middle of the range and then compare x to element number mid of the table. If x is less than this element, then mid is now the lowest subscript beyond the range; we therefore set $hi = mid$. If x is greater, then *mid* +1 is now the lowest subscript of the reduced range; we therefore set *lo=mid* +1. Finally, if *x* is equal to the element, we're done.

Is it good enough to set *mid* =(*hi* +*lo*)/2? There is clearly no problem if *hi* and *lo* are far apart, but what if they are close together?

The case *hi=lo* is not a problem; we already know the range is empty and therefore we never bother setting *mid*. The case *hi=lo* +2 is also not a problem: *hi* +*lo* is then equal to 2×*lo*+2, which is an even number, so (*hi* +*lo*)/2 is equal to *lo* +1. What about *hi=lo* +1? In that case, the only element in the range is element number *lo*, so it would be nice if (*hi* +*lo*)/2=*lo*.

Fortunately this is true because *hi* +*lo* is always positive; division in that case is guaranteed to truncate down. Thus (*hi* +*lo*)/2 is equivalent to ((*lo* +1)+*lo*)/2 or (2×*lo*+1)/2, which is just *lo*.

The program therefore looks like this:

```
int *
bsearch(int *t, int n, int x)
{
        int lo = 0, hi = n;
        while (lo < hi) {
                int mid = (lo + hi) / 2;
                if (x < t[mid])
                        hi = mid;
                else if (x > t[mid])
                        lo = mid + 1;
                else
                        return t + mid;
        }
        return NULL;
}
```

Notice that evaluating

```
int mid = (lo + hi) / 2;
```

involves a division that can be written instead as a shift:

```
int mid = (lo + hi) >> 1;
```

This will indeed speed up the program. First, though, let's try to get rid of some of the address arithmetic; subscript operations are slower than pointer operations on many machines. We can reduce address arithmetic slightly by storing t+mid in a local variable instead of recalculating it:

```
int *
bsearch(int *t, int n, int x)
{
        int lo = 0, hi = n;
        while (lo < hi) {
                int mid = (lo + hi) / 2;
                int *p = t + mid;
                if (x < *p)
                        hi = mid;
                else if (x > *p)
                        lo = mid + 1;
                else
                        return p;
        }
        return NULL;
}
```

Suppose we want to reduce address arithmetic still further by using pointers instead of subscripts throughout the program. It would seem at first glance that we can just rewrite it systematically:

```
int *
bsearch(int *t, int n, int x)
{
        int *lo = t, *hi = t + n;
        while (lo < hi) {
                int *mid = (lo + hi) / 2;
                if (x < *mid)
                        hi = mid;
                else if (x > *mid)
                        lo = mid + 1;
                else
                        return mid;
        }
        return NULL;
}
```

Indeed, this almost works. The problem is that the statement

```
mid = (hi + lo) / 2;
```

is illegal because it attempts to add two pointers. We need to calculate the distance between lo and hi and then add half that distance to lo:

```
mid = lo + (hi - lo) / 2;
```

Calculating hi-lo involves a division, but most implementations will be clever enough to implement it as a shift. They won't be clever enough to change our division by 2 into a shift, though: for all the compiler knows, hi-lo might be negative, in which case shifting and dividing by 2 give different answers. Thus we really should write the shift ourselves:

```
mid = lo + (hi - lo) >> 1;
```

Unfortunately, this is still not right. Remember that shift operations bind less tightly than arithmetic! Thus, we must write

```
mid = lo + ((hi - lo) >> 1);
```

and the completed program looks like this:

```
int *
bsearch(int *t, int n, int x)
{
        int *lo = t, *hi = t + n;
        while (lo < hi) {
                int *mid = lo + ((hi - lo) >> 1);
                if (x < *mid)
                        hi = mid;
                else if (x > *mid)
                        lo = mid + 1;
                else
                        return mid;
        }
        return NULL;
}
```

Incidentally, binary searches are often expressed with symmetric bounds. The resulting program looks somewhat neater because of the symmetry:

```
int *
bsearch(int *t, int n, int x)
{
        int lo = 0, hi = n - 1;
        while (lo <= hi) {
                int mid = (lo + hi) / 2;
                if (x < t[mid])
                        hi = mid - 1;
                else if (x > t[mid])
                        lo = mid + 1;
                else
                        return t + mid;
        }
        return NULL;
}
```

However, we run into trouble if we try to translate this program into the "pure pointer" form. The problem is that we cannot just initialize hi to t+n-1 because t+n-1 is an invalid address if n is zero! Thus if we wish to go the pointer route, we must put in a separate test for $n=0$. This argues again for asymmetric bounds.

4–1 Suppose a program contains the declaration

        long foo;

in one file and

        extern short foo;

in another. Suppose further that assigning a small value, say 37, to the long version of foo results in giving the short version the value 37 as well. What likely inference follows about the hardware? What if the short version becomes 0 instead?

If putting 37 in the long also puts 37 in the short, that suggests that the short occupies the same memory as the part of the long that contains the significant bits of 37. It might be that long and short are really the same type, but it is a rare C implementation for which that is true. It is more likely that the low-order bits of a long are in the part of the long that would share space with the short. This is normally the part at the lowest memory address; the likely inference is therefore that we are on a *little-endian* machine. Similarly, if storing 37 in the long sets the short to 0, we are probably on a *big-endian* machine.

4–2 Here's one of the incorrect programs from Section 4.4 (page 61) after simplification:

```
#include <stdio.h>

main()
{
        printf("%g\n", sqrt(2));
}
```

On some systems, this will print

        %g

Why?

Some C implementations have two versions of printf, one of which implements the floating-point format items %e, %f, and %g and the other of which does not. This duplication in the library saves space in programs that don't use floating-point arithmetic because such programs can use the version of printf without floating-point support.

In some systems, the programmer must explicitly tell the linker whether floating-point arithmetic is being used. Others try to decide automatically by having the compiler tell the linker if it sees any floating-point operations in the program.

This program does no floating-point operations! It doesn't include math.h or declare sqrt, so the compiler has no way to know that sqrt is a floating-point function. It didn't even pass a floating-point argument to sqrt. Thus the compiler is justified in telling the linker that this isn't a floating-point program!

What about the sqrt function? Surely the fact that sqrt was fetched from the library is enough evidence that the program does floating-point computation? That is true, of course, but the linker may have decided what version of printf to use before fetching sqrt from the library.

5-1   When a program terminates abnormally, the last few lines of its output are often lost. Why? What can be done about it?

A program that terminates abnormally may not have the opportunity to flush its output buffers. Thus the program may have generated output that is sitting in memory somewhere and was never written out. On some systems, this output may be several pages long.

Losing output this way can mislead people trying to debug such programs, because it gives the impression that the program failed much earlier than it actually did. The solution is to force output to be unbuffered when debugging. The exact incantation for this varies slightly from one system to another but usually looks something like this:

```
setbuf(stdout, (char *) 0);
```

This must be executed before anything is written to stdout, including any calls to printf. A good place for it is as the first statement in the main program.

5-2   The following program copies its input to its output:

```
#include <stdio.h>

main()
{
        register int c;

        while ((c = getchar()) != EOF)
                putchar(c);
}
```

Removing the #include statement from this program causes it to fail to compile because EOF is undefined. It is poor practice to do this, but suppose we define EOF by hand:

```
#define EOF -1

main()
{
        register int c;

        while ((c = getchar()) != EOF)
                putchar(c);
}
```

This program still works on many systems, but on some it runs much more slowly. Why?

Function calls can take a long time, so getchar is often implemented as a macro. This macro is defined in stdio.h, so if a program fails to include stdio.h, the compiler has no way of knowing about the definition of getchar. It therefore assumes that getchar is a function that returns an int.

Many C implementations actually have a getchar function in their libraries, partly to defend against precisely such carelessness and partly for the convenience of people who might want to take the address of getchar. Thus the effect of failing to include stdio.h is to replace the macro version of getchar by a call to the function version. The program becomes slower because of function call overhead. Precisely the same argument applies to putchar.

6—1 Write a macro version of max with integer arguments that evaluates its arguments only once.

The value of each argument to max is potentially used twice: once to compare it and once to use it as the result. Thus it is essential to store each argument in a temporary variable.

Unfortunately, there is no direct way to declare a temporary variable inside a C expression, so if the max macro is to be used in an expression, the variables must be declared elsewhere, probably next to the macro definition instead of as part of it. We make the temporary variables static to avoid name clashes if max is used in more than one program file. Presumably these definitions would appear in some header file:

```
static int max_temp1, max_temp2;
#define max(p,q) (max_temp1=(p),max_temp2=(q), \
        max_temp1>max_temp2? max_temp1: max_temp2)
```

This will work as long as calls to max are not nested; making it work in that case may be impossible.

6–2 Can the "expression"

    (x) ((x)-1)

mentioned in Section 6.1 (page 78) ever be a valid C expression?

One possibility is if **x** is a type name, such as might be defined by

    typedef int x;

In that case,

    (x) ((x)-1)

is equivalent to

    (int) ((int)-1)

which takes the constant –1 and casts it to int twice. The same effect could be achieved by using the preprocessor to define x as a type:

    #define x int

Another possibility arises if **x** is a function pointer. Recall that if a function pointer is used in a context where a function is required, the function addressed by that pointer is automatically fetched and used instead. Thus it is possible to interpret this expression as calling the function pointed to by **x** with (x)-1 as its argument. In order for (x)-1 to be a valid expression, **x** must really point to an element of an array of pointers to functions.

What is the full type of **x**? For convenience, let **T** be the type of **x**, so we can declare **x** by saying

    T x;

Apparently, **x** must be a pointer to a function whose argument is of type T. This makes **T** a little hard to define. The obvious approach doesn't work:

    typedef void (*T)(T);

because T isn't defined until after the declaration is seen! However, it isn't quite necessary to insist that **x** point to a function with a T argument; instead its argument can be any type to which a T can be cast. In particular, void * will work:

    typedef void (*T)(void *);

The point of this exercise is to show that it isn't always possible to dismiss out of hand strange-looking constructs as errors.

7–1   Section 7.3 (page 89) said that a machine with 8-bit characters
would be most likely to have 16-bit or 32-bit integers. Why?

Some computers assign a unique memory address to each character, while
others address memory in words. Word-addressed machines often have
problems processing character data efficiently: getting a single character
from memory entails fetching an entire word and then discarding the
unwanted parts of it.

The efficiency of character processing on character-addressed
machines has caused them to become more popular than word-addressed
machines in recent years. However, the notion of a word is still important to character-addressed machines for integer arithmetic. Since characters are stored in consecutive memory locations, the addresses of consecutive words must differ by the number of characters in a word.

It is much easier for the hardware to convert from character addresses
to word addresses if the number of characters in a word is a power of 2,
because multiplication by a power of 2 is just a shift. Thus it is reasonable to expect a word to be a power of 2 characters long.

Why not 64-bit integers? They would definitely be useful sometimes.
However, they become less important on machines with floating-point
hardware, and they are expensive to implement when compared with
how often that much integer precision is really needed. It is possible to
simulate 64-bit (or longer) integers in software efficiently enough for
occasional use.

7–2   Write a portable version of the atol function, which takes a
pointer to a null-terminated character string as its argument and
returns the corresponding long value. Assume:

- The input will always represent a valid long integer, so atol
  need not check for the input being out of bounds;

- The only valid input characters are digits and + and – signs.
  The input ends at the first invalid character.

We will assume that digits are contiguous in the machine's collating
sequence: every modern machine behaves this way and ANSI C requires
it. The main problem is thus to avoid overflow in intermediate results
even though the final result is in range.

As in the case of printnum, this may be tricky if the most negative
and most positive long values do not match. In particular, if we develop
the value as a positive number and then negate it later, we will overflow
on the most negative integer on many machines.

The following version avoids these overflows by using only negative (and zero) values to build its result:

```
long
atol(char *s)
{
        long r = 0;
        int neg = 0;

        switch (*s) {
        case '-':
                neg = 1;
                /* no break */
        case '+':
                s++;
                break;
        }

        while (*s >= '0' && *s <= '9') {
                int n = *s++ - '0';
                if (neg)
                        n = -n;
                r = r * 10 + n;
        }

        return r;
}
```

APPENDIX: **PRINTF, VARARGS, AND STDARG**

This appendix describes three common C facilities that are often misunderstood: the `printf` family of library functions and the `varargs` and `stdarg` facilities for writing functions with arguments whose number and type vary from one call to another. I often see programs using aspects of `printf` that disappeared years ago and other programs, even production programs, using assorted nonportable kludges to accomplish what they could have done much more cleanly using `varargs` or `stdarg`.

A.1 The `printf` family

The following program is similar to the first C example in Chapter 0:

```
#include <stdio.h>

main()
{
        printf("Hello world\n");
}
```

The output from this program is

```
Hello world
```

followed by a newline character (\n).

The first argument to `printf` is a *format*, a character string that describes the form of the output. Following the normal C convention, this character string must end with a null character (\0); writing the string as a constant automatically guarantees proper termination.

The `printf` function copies characters from the format to the standard output until either the end of the format is reached or a % character is encountered. Instead of printing a % it finds in the format, `printf` looks at a few characters following the % for instructions as to how to convert its next argument. The converted argument is printed in place of the % and the next few characters. Since the format in the example above does not contain a %, the output from `printf` is exactly those characters given in the format. The format, along with its corresponding arguments, determines every character in the output, *including the newline that ends each line*.

The `printf` function has two relatives, `fprintf` and `sprintf`. Where `printf` writes on the standard output, `fprintf` can write on any output file. The specific file to be used is given to `fprintf` as its first argument: it must be a `FILE` pointer. Thus,

        printf(*stuff*);

and

        fprintf(stdout, *stuff*);

mean the same thing.

The `sprintf` function is used when the output is to go somewhere other than to a file. The first argument to `sprintf` is a pointer to a character vector in which `sprintf` will place its output. It is the programmer's responsibility to ensure that this array is large enough to contain the output that `sprintf` will generate. The remaining arguments are identical to those of `printf`. The output of `sprintf` is always terminated by a null character; the only way a null character can appear otherwise is by explicitly using the %c format item to print it.

All three functions return the number of characters transmitted. In the case of `sprintf`, the count does not include the null character at the end of the output. If `printf` or `fprintf` encounter an I/O error while attempting to write, it will return some negative value. In this case, it will be impossible to determine how many characters were written. Since `sprintf` does no I/O, it should never return a negative value (but no doubt some implementation will come up with a reason for it to do so).

Because the format string determines the types of the remaining arguments, and because the format string can be built during execution, it is very hard for a C implementation to check that `printf` arguments are of the right types. Thus saying

        printf("%d\n", 0.1);

or

        printf("%g\n", 2);

will result in garbage and is extremely unlikely to be detected before the program is actually run.

Most implementations miss this one too:

```
fprintf("error\n");
```

The programmer here used `fprintf` intending to write a message on `stderr` but forgot to mention `stderr`; the likely result is a core dump as `fprintf` interprets the format string as a file structure.

Simple format types

Every format item is introduced by a % sign, which is followed, not always immediately, by a character called the *format code*, which gives the type of conversion. Other characters may optionally appear between the % and the format code; they serve to modify the conversion in ways that are detailed later. The format code always ends the format item.

The most common format item is surely %d, which prints an integer value in decimal form. For example,

```
printf("2 + 2 = %d\n", 2 + 2);
```

will print

```
2 + 2 = 4
```

followed by a newline (future examples will not explicitly state the presence of a newline in the output).

The %d format item is a request to print an integer. There must be a corresponding `int` argument. The decimal value of the integer, with no leading or trailing spaces, replaces the %d as the format is copied to the output. If the integer is negative, the first character of the output value is a – sign.

The %u format item treats an integer as if it were `unsigned`. Thus, for example,

```
printf("%u\n", -37);
```

prints

```
4294967259
```

on a machine with 32-bit `int` values.

Recall that `char` and `short` arguments are automatically widened to `int`. This can cause surprises on machines that treat `char` values as signed. For example, on such a machine,

```
char c;

c = -37;
printf("%u\n", c);
```

prints

4294967259

because the char −37 is converted to an int −37. To avoid this problem, reserve the %u format item for unsigned values.

The %o, %x, and %X format items print integer values in base 8 or 16. The %o item requests octal output, and the %x and %X items both request hexadecimal output. The only difference between %x and %X is that the %x item uses the letters a, b, c, d, e, and f for digit values from 10 through 15, and the %X item uses A, B, C, D, E, and F. Octal and hex values are always unsigned.

An example:

```
int n = 108;
printf("%d decimal = %o octal = %x hex\n", n, n, n);
```

prints

```
108 decimal = 154 octal = 6c hex
```

If %X were used instead of %x, the output would be

```
108 decimal = 154 octal = 6C hex
```

The %s format item prints strings: the corresponding argument must be a character pointer, and characters are printed starting at the location addressed by the argument until a null character ('\0') is encountered. Here is one way to use a %s format item:

```
printf("There %s %d item%s in the list.\n",
       n!=1? "are": "is", n, n!=1? "s": "");
```

Either is or are will be substituted for the first %s, and either s or the null string will be substituted for the second %s. Thus if n is 37, the output will be

```
There are 37 items in the list.
```

but if n is 1, the output will be

```
There is 1 item in the list.
```

A string printed with the %s format item *must* be terminated by a null character ('\0') (with one exception to be covered later). That is the only way that printf can find the end of the string. If a string that is given to the %s item is not properly terminated, printf will continue printing characters until it finds a '\0' somewhere in memory — the output may be very long indeed!

Since the %s format item prints every character in the corresponding argument,

```
    printf(s);
```

and

```
    printf("%s", s);
```

do not mean the same thing. The first example will treat any % character in s as beginning a format code; this will cause trouble if any format codes other than %% appear because there is no corresponding argument. The second example will print any null-terminated string.

Since a NULL pointer does not point anywhere, it certainly does not point to a string of characters. Hence the results of

```
    printf("%s\n", NULL);
```

are unpredictable. Section 3.5 (page 35) discusses this in more detail.

The %c format item prints a single character:

```
    printf("%c", c);
```

is equivalent to

```
    putchar(c);
```

but has the added flexibility of being able to embed the value of the character c in some larger context. The argument that corresponds to a %c format item is an int that is converted to a char for printing. For example:

```
    printf("The decimal equivalent of '%c' is %d\n",
           '*', '*');
```

will print

```
    The decimal equivalent of '*' is 42
```

Three format items print floating-point values: %g, %f, and %e. The %g format item is the most useful for printing floating-point values that are not to appear in columns. It causes the corresponding value (which must be float or double) to be printed, with trailing zeroes removed, to six significant digits. Thus, after including math.h,

```
    printf("Pi = %g\n", 4 * atan(1.0));
```

prints

```
    Pi = 3.14159
```

and

```
    printf("%g %g %g %g %g\n",
           1/1.0, 1/2.0, 1/3.0, 1/4.0, 0.0);
```

prints

    1 0.5 0.333333 0.25 0

Leading zeroes do not contribute to the precision, so there are six 3s in
0.333333. Values printed are rounded, not truncated:

    printf("%g\n", 2.0 / 3.0);

prints

    0.666667

If the magnitude is greater than 999999, printing the value in the format
just described would require either printing more than six significant
digits or displaying an incorrect value. The %g format item resolves this
problem by printing such a value in scientific notation:

    printf("%g\n", 123456789.0);

prints

    1.23457e+08

The value is again rounded to six significant digits.

    When the magnitude gets small enough, the number of characters
required to represent the value gets uncomfortably large. For example, it
is ungainly to write $\pi \times 10^{-10}$ as 0.000000000314159; it is both more
compact and easier to read if written as 3.14159e-10. These two forms
have the same length whenever the exponent is exactly −4 (for example:
0.000314159 takes as much space as 3.14159e-04); the %g format item
therefore does not start to use scientific notation for small numbers until
the exponent is −5 or smaller. Thus

    printf("%g %g %g\n", 3.14159e-3, 3.14159e-4, 3.14159e-5);

prints

    0.00314159 0.000314159 3.14159e-05

The %e format item insists on writing floating-point values with an
explicit exponent: π written under %e format is 3.141593e+00. The %e
format item prints six digits *after the decimal point*, rather than six significant digits.

    The %f format item forces the value to be printed *without* an explicit
exponent, so π appears as 3.141593. Again, the %f format item prints
six digits after the decimal point. Thus a very small value may appear as
zero even if it is not, and a very large value appears with a lot of digits:

    printf("%f\n", 1e38);

prints

10000000000000000000000000000000000000.000000

Since the number of digits printed here exceeds the precision of most hardware, the result may vary on different machines.

The %E and %G format items behave in the same way as their lower-case counterparts, except that E instead of e will introduce the exponent.

The %% format item prints a % character. It is unique in that it is used *without* a corresponding argument. Thus, the statement

```
printf("%%d prints a decimal value\n");
```

prints

```
%d prints a decimal value
```

Modifiers

The printf function accepts additional characters that modify the meaning of a format item. These characters appear between the % and the following format code.

Integers come in three lengths: short, long, and plain. If a short integer appears as an argument to any function, including printf, it is automatically expanded to a plain integer, but we still need a way to tell printf to expect a long argument. This is done by inserting an l immediately before the format code, creating %ld, %lo, %lx, and %lu as new format codes. These modified codes behave in exactly the same way as their unmodified counterparts, except that they demand a long integer to correspond with them. The %lu format item prints a long integer as if it were long unsigned even in those few C implementations that do not support long unsigned values directly. The l modifier is meaningful only for integer format codes.

Many implementations store int and long values with the same precision. Failure to use an l modifier on such a machine will go undetected until the program is moved to a machine in which int and long are truly different. Thus, for example,

```
long size;
. . .
printf("%d\n", size);
```

will work on some machines and not others.

The *width modifier* makes it easier to print values in fixed-width fields. It appears between the % and the following format code, and specifies the *minimum* number of characters that should be printed by the format item it modifies. If the value being printed does not fill the field, blanks will be added on the left to make the value wide enough. If the value printed is too big for the field, the field is expanded appropriately. *The width modifier never causes truncation of a field.* When using the width modifier to line up columns of figures, a value that is too large for its column will displace subsequent values on that row to the right.

This program fragment:

```
int i;
for (i = 0; i <= 10; i++)
        printf("%2d %2d *\n", i, i * i);
```

produces the following output:

```
 0   0 *
 1   1 *
 2   4 *
 3   9 *
 4  16 *
 5  25 *
 6  36 *
 7  49 *
 8  64 *
 9  81 *
10 100 *
```

The * in this example marks the end of the line. The value 100 is too large to fit in two characters, so its field is expanded and the rest of the line shifted right.

The width modifier is effective for all format codes, even %%. Thus, for example,

```
printf("%8%\n");
```

prints a % right-justified in an eight-character field. In other words, it prints seven spaces followed by a %.

The *precision* modifier controls the number of digits that appear in the representation of a number or limits the number of characters printed from a string. It consists of a decimal point followed by a string of digits and appears before the format code and length modifier and after the % and width modifier. The exact meaning of the precision modifier varies with the format code:

- For the integer format items %d, %o, %x, and %u, it specifies the *minimum* number of digits to print. If the value doesn't need that many digits, leading zeroes will be supplied. Thus,

```
printf("%.2d/%.2d/%.4d\n", 7, 14, 1789);
```

prints

07/14/1789

- For %e, %E, and %f format items, the precision specifies the number of digits after the decimal point. Unless the flags (which we will discuss shortly) specify otherwise, a decimal point appears only if the precision is greater than zero. Thus, after including math.h,

```
double pi;
pi = 4 * atan(1.0);
printf("%.0f %.1f %.2f %.3f %.6f %.10f\n",
        pi, pi, pi, pi, pi, pi);
printf("%.0e %.1e %.2e %.10e\n",
        pi, pi, pi, pi, pi, pi);
```

prints

```
3 3.1 3.14 3.142 3.141593 3.1415926536
3e+00 3.1e+00 3.14e+00 3.1415926536e+00
```

- For %g and %G format items, the precision specifies the number of *significant digits* to print. Unless the flags specify otherwise, insignificant zeroes are removed, and the decimal point is deleted if no digits follow it.

```
printf("%.1g %.2g %.4g %.8g\n",
        10/3.0, 10/3.0, 10/3.0, 10/3.0);
```

produces

```
3 3.3 3.333 3.3333333
```

- For %s format items, the precision gives the number of characters to print from the corresponding string. If the string doesn't have enough characters to satisfy the precision, the output will be shorter than that; the field width modifier can lengthen the output if needed.

Some systems store a filename component in a 14-character array. If the component name has fewer than 14 characters, the remainder of the array is filled with null characters, but if the name has its maximum length, no null character terminates the array. Such a name might be printed as follows:

```
char name[14];
  . . .
printf("... %.14s ...", ... , name, ...);
```

This ensures that the name is printed properly, regardless of its length. Using a format item of %14.14s would guarantee that exactly 14 characters would be printed, regardless of the length of the name (if necessary, the name will be padded on the *left* to 14 characters; we will see shortly how to pad it on the right).

- The precision is ignored for c and % format items.

Flags

Between the % and the field width, characters may appear that alter the effect of the format item slightly. These are called *flag characters*. The flag characters and their meanings are as follows:

- The – flag is meaningful only if a width is present (because padding is only necessary if the width is greater than necessary to contain the value printed). In that case, any padding blanks will appear on the right rather than on the left.

  When printing character strings in fixed columns, it usually looks better to left-justify them. Thus a format like %14s is probably a mistake and should have been written as %–14s. The previous example therefore probably gives more attractive results this way:

  ```
  char name[14];
      . . .
  printf("... %-14s ...", ... , name, ...);
  ```

- The + flag specifies that every numeric value printed should have a sign as its first character. Thus nonnegative values will appear with a + as the first character. It bears no relationship to the – flag.

  ```
  printf("%+d %+d %+d\n", -5, 0, 5);
  ```

  produces

  ```
  -5 +0 +5
  ```

- When a blank is used as a flag, it means that a single blank is to appear before a numeric value if its first character is not a sign. This is most useful for making left-justified columns of numbers line up without using + signs. If the + and blank flags appear with the same format item, the + flag takes precedence. For example,

  ```
  int i;
  for (i = -3; i <= 3; i++)
          printf("% d\n", i);
  ```

  prints

```
-3
-2
-1
 0
 1
 2
 3
```

The `%  e` and `%+e` format items are more useful than the plain `%e` format item for printing numbers in columns in scientific notation: the presence of the sign (or blank) in all output values guarantees that the decimal points will all line up. For example:

```
double x;

for (x = -3; x <= 3; x++)
        printf("% e  %+e  %e\n", x, x, x);
```

prints

```
-3.000000e+00   -3.000000e+00   -3.000000e+00
-2.000000e+00   -2.000000e+00   -2.000000e+00
-1.000000e+00   -1.000000e+00   -1.000000e+00
 0.000000e+00   +0.000000e+00    0.000000e+00
 1.000000e+00   +1.000000e+00    1.000000e+00
 2.000000e+00   +2.000000e+00    2.000000e+00
 3.000000e+00   +3.000000e+00    3.000000e+00
```

The column printed with `%e` doesn't line up correctly, but the other two do.

- The `#` flag alters the format of numeric values slightly, in a way that depends on the particular format item. Its effect on the `%o` format item is to increase the precision, if necessary, just enough that the first digit that is printed is 0. The idea is to permit octal values to be printed in the format in which most C programmers are used to seeing them. `%#o` is not the same as `0%o` because `0%o` prints zero as `00`. Similarly, the `%#x` and `%#X` format items cause the value to be preceded by `0x` and `0X`, respectively.

The `#` flag affects floating-point formats in two ways: it causes the decimal point always to be printed, even if there are no digits after it; and it stops the `%g` and `%G` formats from suppressing trailing zeroes. For example,

```
printf("%.0f %#.0f %g %#g\n",
        3.0, 3.0, 3.0, 3.0);
```

produces

```
        3 3.  3 3.00000
```

The flags are all independent of each other, except for blank and +.

Variable field width and precision

A number of C programs carefully define the width of some character array as a manifest constant to make it easy to change but then state the width as an integer constant when it comes time to print it. Thus our earlier example might be unwisely rewritten this way:

```
#define NAMESIZE 14
char name[NAMESIZE];
   . . .
printf("... %.14s ...", ... , name, ...);
```

The purpose of defining NAMESIZE was to make it unnecessary to mention the value 14 more than once; someone changing NAMESIZE later is likely to forget to search every printf call for values to change. Yet it is not possible to use NAMESIZE directly in a printf call:

```
printf("... %.NAMESIZE ...", ... , name, ...);
```

won't work because the preprocessor won't reach inside strings.

The printf function therefore allows a field width or precision to be given indirectly. To do this, replace either or both of the field width and precision by a *. In this case, printf takes the actual value(s) to be used from its argument list before it fetches the value to be printed. Thus the example above could be written

```
printf("... %.*s ...", ... , NAMESIZE, name, ...);
```

If the * convention is used for both field width and precision, the field width argument appears first, followed by the precision argument and then by the value to be printed. Thus

```
printf("%*.*s\n", 12, 5, str);
```

has the same effect as

```
printf("%12.5s\n", str);
```

which prints the first five characters of str (or fewer, if strlen(s) < 5), preceded by enough blanks to bring the total number of characters printed to 12. As an arcane example,

```
printf("%*%\n", n);
```

prints a % right-justified in a field of n characters; this is equivalent to $n-1$ spaces followed by a %.

If * is used for the field width, and the corresponding value is negative, the effect is as if the − flag were also present. Thus, in the example immediately above, if *n* is negative, the output will be a % *followed* by 1−*n* spaces.

Neologisms

The ANSI definition has added two new format codes: %p prints a pointer in some form that is suitable for the particular C implementation, and %n indicates how many characters have been printed so far by *storing* a value into the int addressed by the corresponding argument. After executing

```
    int n;

    printf("hello\n%n", &n);
```

n has the value 6.

Anachronisms

Several things have vanished from printf over the years. Some implementations still support them.

The %D and %O format items were once synonyms for %ld and %lo. Moreover, the %X format item was a synonym for %lx. It was considered more useful to be able to print hex values in upper case, so the meaning of %X changed. %D and %O were dropped at the same time.

At one time, the only way to print a value with leading zeroes was to use 0 as a flag. This would indicate that the value printed should be padded with zeroes instead of blanks. Thus

```
    printf("%06d %06d\n", -37, 37);
```

would print

```
    -00037 000037
```

However, the definition of this interacted strangely with requests for left justification and printing hex values. The precision modifier for integers is therefore a much better way to do this:

```
    printf("%.6d %.6d\n", -37, 37);
```

prints

```
    -000037 000037
```

which is close enough that %. can be substituted for %0 in most contexts.

A.2 Variable argument lists with varargs.h

As a C program grows, its author will often want to systematize error handling. A natural way to do this is to have a function called, say, error, with the same kind of calling sequence as printf, so that

```
error("%d is out of bounds", x);
```

has the same effect as

```
fprintf(stderr, "error: %d is out of bounds\n", x);
exit(1);
```

Such a function is trivial to implement except for one little detail: the number and types of arguments to error will differ from one call to another, just as they do for printf. A typical, but incorrect, way to cope with this problem is to make the error function look something like this:

```
void error(a, b, c, d, e, f, g, h, i, j, k)
{
        fprintf(stderr, "error: ");
        fprintf(stderr, a, b, c, d, e, f, g, h, i, j, k);
        fprintf(stderr, "\n");
        exit(1);
}
```

The idea is to gather a bunch of data from the argument list and pass it on to fprintf; since the arguments a through k are not declared, they are assumed to be int values. Of course, the arguments to error will always include at least one non-int (the format string), so this program relies on being able to use a series of int arguments to copy values of arbitrary type.

This will fail on some machines. Even when it succeeds, it is limited: if error has enough arguments, some of them will surely be lost. And yet it must be possible to pass a variable argument list to a function somehow because every program that calls printf does it.

One thing gives printf an easier job: its first argument must be a character string, and by inspecting this string it is possible to derive the number and types of the other arguments (assuming, of course, that the call to printf is correctly coded). What we need is a way to get at whatever mechanism printf uses to access variable-length argument lists.

Such a mechanism must have the following characteristics to allow printf to be implemented:

- The first argument to a function can be accessed knowing only its type.

- Once argument n has been successfully accessed, argument $n+1$ can be accessed knowing only its type.

- The time required to access an argument this way should not be excessive.

Note in particular that it is not necessary to be able to access arguments backwards, or in random order, or in any order other than sequentially from the first one. Moreover, in general it is neither necessary nor possible to detect the end of the argument list.

Most C implementations achieve this through a set of macro definitions collectively called **varargs**. The exact nature of these macros will vary from one implementation to another, but a program that uses them carefully will be able to use variable argument lists on a wide variety of machines.

Every program that uses **varargs** must fetch the relevant macro definitions by saying

```
#include <varargs.h>
```

This header file defines the names `va_list`, `va_dcl`, `va_start`, `va_end`, and `va_arg`. The programmer is expected to define `va_alist`; we shall see how shortly. It is important to avoid confusing `va_list` and `va_alist`.

For each C implementation, there is some information that is needed to access argument n of a variable argument list if its type is known. This information is derived as a side effect of having accessed arguments 1 through $n-1$, and may be thought of as a pointer into the argument list, although its implementation may be considerably more complex on some machines.

This information is stored in an object of type `va_list`. Thus, after declaring a `va_list` named `ap`, it will be possible to determine the value of the first argument given only `ap` and the type of the first argument.

Accessing an argument through a `va_list` will also advance that `va_list` to refer to the next argument in the list.

Because a `va_list` contains *all* the information necessary to access *all* the arguments, a function f can create a `va_list` for its arguments and pass it to another function g, which can then step through the arguments of f.

For example in many implementations, each of the three `printf` functions calls a common sub-function, and it is important for this sub-function to be able to scan its caller's arguments.

A function that is called with a variable argument list must use the va_alist and va_dcl macros to form the beginning of its definition, as follows:

```
#include <varargs.h>

void error (va_alist) va_dcl
```

The va_alist macro expands into the argument list that the particular implementation will require to allow the function to handle a varying number of arguments, and the va_dcl macro expands into the declarations appropriate to the argument list, *including* a terminating semicolon if necessary.

To scan its argument list, our error function must create a va_list variable and initialize it by passing its name to the macro va_start. Once the program is done with the argument list, it must call va_end with the va_list name as its argument, to indicate that it no longer needs the va_list.

Our error function has grown:

```
#include <varargs.h>

void error(va_alist) va_dcl
{
        va_list ap;
        va_start(ap);

        the part of the program that uses ap appears here

        va_end(ap);

        other stuff may appear here, as long as it doesn't use ap
}
```

It is important to remember to call va_end. It makes no difference in most C implementations, but a few versions of va_start allocate dynamic storage for a copy of the argument list to make it easier to traverse. Such an implementation is likely to use va_end to free that storage; forgetting to call va_end may therefore result in a program that appears to work fine on some machines but slowly eats memory on others.

The va_arg macro is used to access an argument. Its two arguments are the name of a va_list and the *data type* of the argument it intends to access next. It fetches the argument and updates the va_list to refer to the next argument. Thus our error function now looks like this:

```
#include <varargs.h>

void error(va_alist) va_dcl
{
        va_list ap;
        char *format;

        va_start(ap);
        format = va_arg(ap, char *);
        fprintf(stderr, "error: ");
```

do something magic

```
        va_end(ap);
        fprintf(stderr, "\n");
        exit(1);
}
```

Now we are stuck: there is no way to get printf to take a va_list as an argument. We need to do that, as indicated by the "do something magic" remark, but how?

Fortunately, many C implementations have, and ANSI C requires, functions called vprintf, vfprintf, and vsprintf. These functions behave like the printf functions except that they take a va_list in place of the list of arguments after the format. These functions can exist only because a va_list can be passed as an argument and a va_arg need not appear in the same function as the call to va_start that established the va_list it uses.

Thus, our final version of error looks like this:

```
#include <stdio.h>
#include <varargs.h>

void error (va_alist) va_dcl
{
        va_list ap;
        char *format;

        va_start(ap);
        format = va_arg(ap, char *);
        fprintf(stderr, "error: ");
        vfprintf(stderr, format, ap);
        va_end(ap);
        fprintf(stderr, "\n");
        exit(1);
}
```

As another example, here is one way to implement printf in terms of

vprintf. Don't forget to save the result of **vprintf** to return to the caller of **printf**:

```
#include <varargs.h>

int
printf(va_alist) va_dcl
{
        va_list ap;
        char *format;
        int n;

        va_start(ap);
        format = va_arg(ap, char *);
        n = vprintf(format, ap);
        va_end(ap);
        return n;
}
```

Implementing varargs.h

A typical implementation of **varargs.h** is all macros, except for a typedef declaration for **va_list**:

```
typedef char *va_list;
#define va_dcl int va_alist;
#define va_start(list) list = (char *) &va_alist
#define va_end(list)
#define va_arg(list,mode) \
        ((mode *) (list += sizeof(mode)))[-1]
```

Note first that **va_alist** is not even a macro in this version:

```
#include <varargs.h>

void error (va_alist) va_dcl
```

expands into:

```
typedef char *va_list;
void error(va_alist) int va_alist;
```

so a function that accepts a variable argument list appears to have a single **int** argument named **va_alist**.

This example assumes an underlying C implementation that stores the arguments for a function in contiguous memory, so that the address of the current argument is all the information needed to step through the arguments. Thus **va_list** is simply a character pointer in this implementation. The **va_start** macro sets its argument to the address of va_alist (with a cast to avoid a complaint from lint), and va_end does nothing at all.

The most complicated macro is va_arg. It must return the value of appropriate type pointed to by its va_list argument, and increment that argument by the length of an object of that type. Since the result of a cast cannot appear as the target of an assignment it accomplishes this by using sizeof to determine an appropriate increment and adding it directly to the va_list. The resulting pointer is cast into the required mode, and, since it now points one increment too far, a subscript of -1 is used to access the correct argument.

A trap to avoid is trying to specify a second argument of char, short, or float to va_arg: char and short arguments are converted to int, and float arguments are converted to double. Incorrect specifications of this sort will cause trouble.

For example, it is never correct to say

```
c = va_arg(ap,char);
```

because there is no way to pass a char argument; such an argument is automatically converted to int. Instead, say

```
c = va_arg(ap,int);
```

On the other hand, if cp is a character pointer and a character pointer argument is expected, it is completely correct to say

```
cp = va_arg(ap,char *);
```

Pointers are not changed when used as arguments, just char, short, and float values.

Note also that there is no built-in way to tell how many arguments were given. It is up to each individual program that uses varargs to establish some convention to mark the end of the argument list. For example, the printf functions use the format string to determine the number and types of the additional arguments.

A.3   stdarg.h: the ANSI varargs.h

The varargs.h facility dates back to 1981 and is therefore available on a variety of C implementations. The ANSI C standard, however, includes a different mechanism, called stdarg.h, for dealing with variable argument lists.

The discussion in Section 7.1 (page 85) is relevant here to both C users and implementers. Including varargs.h as an extension in an ANSI C compiler is an excellent idea in order to make it possible to run older programs. Thus in practice, using varargs.h is likely to result in a

program that will run on more systems than a comparable program using
stdarg.h. But if you want to write an ANSI conforming program, you
must use stdarg.h: you have no choice! This is one of those trouble-
some situation when every alternative costs something.

The main difference between varargs.h and stdarg.h stems from
the observation that in practice the *first* argument to a function must be
the same type in every call. A function like printf can determine the
type of its second argument by examining its first argument, but there is
no information from its argument list that it can use to find the type of
its first argument. Therefore, a function that uses stdarg.h must have
at least one argument of fixed type, followed by an unknown number of
arguments of unknown type.

As an example, let's look at the error function again. Its first argument is a printf format, which is always a character pointer. Thus the
function can be declared this way:

```
void error(char *, ...);
```

What about the definition of error? The stdarg.h facility doesn't use
the va_arg or va_dcl macros of varargs.h. Instead, a function that
uses stdarg.h declares its fixed parameters directly and uses them as the
basis for its variable arguments by making the last fixed parameter an
argument to va_start. Thus error is defined this way:

```
#include <stdio.h>
#include <stdarg.h>

void error(char *format, ...)
{
        va_list ap;
        va_start(ap, format);
        fprintf(stderr, "error: ");
        vfprintf(stderr, format, ap);
        va_end(ap);
        fprintf(stderr, "\n");
        exit(1);
}
```

There is no need to use va_arg in this example because the format string
is in the fixed part of the argument list.

As another example, here is how to use stdarg.h to write printf in
terms of vprintf:

```
#include <stdarg.h>

int
printf(char *format, ...)
{
        va_list ap;
        int n;

        va_start(ap, format);
        n = vprintf(format, ap);
        va_end(ap);
        return n;
}
```

INDEX

%% 127, 130
+ 130
# 131
* 18
++ 18
!= 19
^ 19
?: 19, 47
; 20
, 20, 47
! 48
~ 48
-> 5
- 5, 130
:= 6
== 6, 8, 19
= 6, 8, 20
&& 7, 19, 47-48
|| 7, 19, 47-48, 83
& 7, 19, 48
| 7, 19, 48
*/ 8
+= 8
-- 8
/* 8
=+ 8
=- 8
=/ 9
>>= 9
<< 90
>> 90
/ 92
% 92, 123
0 124

Ada 6
airplane v
Algol 6
Algol 68 25
anachronism 133
analysis, greedy lexical 7
analyzer, lexical 5
anonymous contributor 22
ANSI C 85, 119
archaicism 8
argument 57
argument list, empty 24
argument list, variable 134-141
arithmetic, integer 49
array 27-46
array bound 48
array parameter 33
assignment 6, 20
assignment, multiple 6
asymmetric bound 36, 48
atol 99
automatic conversions 59

B programming language 19
Bellovin, Steve 82
big-endian 115
binary operator 18
blank (used as flag) 130
bound, array 48
bound, asymmetric 36, 48
Brader, Mark 6
break 22
buffered output 72

bufwrite 40

%c 125, 130
call, function 18
Cardelli, Luca 62
case conversion 93–95
cast 14
change, coping with 85
char 89
character 10
character, null 121, 124
character, signed 89
character, unsigned 89
checking, type 63
Cipriani, Larry 21
code, format 123
comma operator 47
comment 8
comment, nested 11
comparison 6
compatibility 85
compilation, separate 53, 59
conditional expression 47
constant, defined 17
constant, integer 9
constant, manifest 77
constant, octal 9
contributor, anonymous 22
conversion, case 93–95
conversions, automatic 59
coping with change 85
counting 36–46

%d 123, 128
dangling else 24
declaration, external 54
declaration, function 13–17
declarator 13
defined constant 17
definition, external 54
definition, macro 77
definition, type 83
division 92

%e 125–126, 129

%E 127, 129
editor, linkage 53
else, dangling 24
empty argument list 24
end of file 70
EOF 70
equality 6
errno 73
error, fencepost 36–46
error, off-by-one 36–46
evaluation, order of 46
example of portability problems 96–99
exit 74
expression, conditional 47
extern 54
external declaration 54
external definition 54
external identifier, length of 87
external name 53
external object 53
external type 63

%f 125–126, 129
false 48
fencepost error 36–46
Feuer, Alan vi
Fibonacci numbers 1
field width, variable 132
file, end of 70
file, header 66
file, updating a 70
flags, format 130
floating-point 125
_flsbuf 80
fopen 70
for statement 38
format code 123
format flags 130
format item 123
format modifier 127
format string 122
Fortran 1
fprintf 122
fread 71
free 95
fseek 71
function 24

function call 18
function declaration 13–17
function, library 69
function, macro used as 78
function prototype 57, 86
fwrite 71

%g 125, 131
%G 127, 131
getchar 70
greedy lexical analysis 7

Harbison, Samuel vi
harpsichord 101
Harris, Guy 20
header file 66
hexadecimal 124
Horton, Mark vi, 85

identifier 5
identifier, length of external 87
include 66
infinite loop 2
integer arithmetic 49
integer constant 9
integer size 88
interpreter 23
item, format 123

Johnson, Steve 20

Karn, Phil 17
Kernighan, Brian vi
Kristol, Dave 90

%ld 127
Leach, George W. 7
length of external identifier 87
lexical analysis, greedy 7
lexical analyzer 5
library function 69
linear search 48

linkage editor 53
linker 53
lint 20, 53
little-endian 115
%lo 127
loader 53
location zero 13, 91
logical operator 19
longjmp 74
loop, infinite 2
%lu 127
%lx 127

macro definition 77
macro used as function 78
macro used as type definition 82
main 50
malloc 32, 73–74, 88, 95
manifest constant 77
math.h 116
maximal munch 8
McIlroy, Doug 21, 106
memcpy 41
mistake, stupid vi
modifier, format 127
modifier, precision 128
modifier, width 127
Moo, Barbara 88
multiple assignment 6
munch, maximal 8

name, external 53
neologism 133
nested comment 11
newline 121–122
null character 121, 124
NULL pointer 125
number, random 93
numbers, Fibonacci 1

%o 124, 128, 131
object, external 53
octal 124
octal constant 9
off-by-one error 36–46

operator 17
operator, binary 18
operator, comma 47
operator, logical 19
operator precedence table 17
operator, shift 90
operator, unary 18
order of evaluation 46
output, buffered 72
overflow 49

parameter 57
parameter, array 33
Pascal 22
Pike, Rob vi, 6, 102
pilot, student v
pitfall see trap
pointer 27–46
pointer, NULL 125
portability 85
portability problems, example of
    96–99
precedence 6–7, 17–20, 78
precedence table, operator 17
precision modifier 128
precision, variable 132
preprocessor 26, 77
printf 10, 62, 121–133
printneg 97–99
printnum 96–99, 119
prompt 2
prototype, function 57, 86
putc 80

quote 10

r+ 70
rand 93
random number 93
read 69
realloc 95
recursion 88, 146
Reeds, Jim 36
remainder 92
result 58

return value 50, 57
Ritchie, Dennis vi, 19

%s 124, 129
scanf 62
search, linear 48
semantics 27
semicolon 20
separate compilation 53, 59
setbuf 72, 116
shift operator 90
signal 15, 74
signed character 89
Sirkis, Janet 70
size, integer 88
sizeof 28–29
space, white 5, 8, 24, 77
sprintf 122
sqrt 116
static 43, 54, 56
stdarg.h 139–141
stderr 122
Steele, Guy vi
Stevens, Richard 24
strcat 32
strcmp 36
strcpy 32
string 10
string, format 122
Stroustrup, Bjarne 20
student pilot v
stupid mistake vi
subscript 48
switch 22
synecdoche 34
syntax 13

table, operator precedence 17
token 5
tolower 93–95
toupper 80, 93–95
training wheels v
trap see pitfall
true 48
truncation 92
type checking 63

type definition 83
type definition, macro used as 82
type, external 63
typedef 15–16, 83, 89

%u 128
unary operator 18
unsigned 71, 90
unsigned character 89
updating a file 70

va_alist 135
va_arg 135
va_dcl 135
va_end 135–136
va_list 135
value, return 50, 57
Van Wyk, Chris vi
varargs.h 134–139
variable argument list 134–141
variable field width 132
variable precision 132
va_start 135–136
vfprintf 137
Vishniac, Ephraim 9
vprintf 137
vsprintf 137

Way, David Jacques 101
wheels, training v
white space 5, 8, 24, 77
width modifier 127
write 69

%X 124, 128
%x 124, 128, 131

zero, location 13, 91